Especially for

_____

From

_____

Date

_____

The Comfort

of

God's Love

Devotions Inspired by the Beloved Classic
The God of All Comfort

BARBOUR

Print ISBN 978-1-62416-857-4

eBook Editions:
Adobe Digital Edition (.epub) 978-1-63058-039-1
Kindle and MobiPocket Edition (.prc) 978-1-63058-040-7

Devotional writing by Marcia Ford in association with Snapdragon Group℠.

Published by Barbour Publishing, Inc., P.O. Box 719, Uhrichsville, Ohio 44683, www.barbourbooks.com

Our mission is to publish and distribute inspirational products offering exceptional value and biblical encouragement to the masses.

Member of the
Evangelical Christian
Publishers Association

Printed in the United States of America.

How would our lives change if we were free of fear, doubt, and despair? What if we could be absolutely certain that we could find comfort and relief from the burdens we bear? It was Hannah Whitall Smith's conviction that our lives would change dramatically if we only understood that God's comfort—His loving compassion that offers the relief we seek from the stresses of everyday life—is available to everyone, all the time.

The one hundred devotions that follow, each based on a passage from Smith's 1906 book *The God of All Comfort*, reflect that conviction. Each reading opens with the passage from Smith's classic *The God of All Comfort* that inspired it. This volume, *The Comfort of God's Love*, has been written to reinforce Smith's desire to see all people find freedom in Christ. Smith, who was dismayed by the demeanor of Christians who led "utterly uncomfortable religious lives," set out to convince her readers that God's care and concern for them was cause for great rejoicing. Drawing on various biblical images of God—as Father, Mother, Shepherd, and the many names of Jehovah, for example—Smith presents a portrait of God as the Creator of the universe who is intimately and lovingly involved in the lives of the people He created.

What is perhaps most surprising about *The God of All Comfort* is its relevance to contemporary readers and especially to the church. Smith carefully dismantles unbiblical teachings that leave some Christians feeling as if they're unworthy and others convinced of their own superiority. In their place, she highlights biblical passages that focus Christians' attention away from themselves, their man-made doctrines, and their church projects, and onto Christ, where their focus belongs.

In fact, while Smith writes a great deal about God's comfort, her overriding message is this: God is enough. All the trappings of church life, the wonderful work of missions and outreach, and the beliefs and practices that people hold so dear are secondary to our praise, worship, and adoration of God. In God alone will we find the answers to the problems we face, relief from the pain we endure, and freedom from the sin that threatens to undo us. He is, after all, the God of all comfort.

The LORD wants to show his mercy to you.
He wants to rise and comfort you.
The LORD is a fair God, and everyone
who waits for his help will be happy.

ISAIAH 30:18 NCV

Knowing Jesus, Knowing God

"Christ revealed God by what He was, by what He did,
and by what He said. From the cradle to the grave,
every moment of His life was a revelation of God.
We must go to Him then for our knowledge of God,
and we must refuse to believe anything concerning God that is
not revealed to us in Christ. Only in Christ do we see God as He is."

*I*t's a question people have asked for millennia: "How can we possibly know God?" After all, God is invisible and doesn't speak in an audible voice. Logical reasoning leads many people to conclude that it's impossible to know someone who can't be seen or heard.

God is well aware of the limitations of human thinking, and He anticipated this very problem at the dawn of creation. Two thousand years ago, He gave the world an exact representation of Himself in the form of a man who was both seen and heard. That man was Jesus.

When Jesus healed the sick, the blind, and the paralyzed, He revealed who God is. When He declared the sinful to now be free of sin, He again revealed who God is. When He denounced the self-righteous and embraced the humble, He revealed even more of God's character. The people of His day saw God in the flesh through the things Jesus did and heard God speak through the words Jesus uttered.

But how does that help those who want to know God today? Jesus is no longer here on earth, walking and talking with people. Fortunately, the historical record is clear: Jesus was as real as anyone who ever lived. He ate and drank and slept and cried—and even cooked breakfast for His friends. He confronted the religious authorities of that time and uncovered their abuses. He spoke to individuals and large crowds alike and attracted a significant following of people who both saw and heard him and never doubted He was a real man.

If we want to know God, we have one clear way to do so: by getting to know Jesus. We do that not only by reading about what He said and did while He was on earth but also by patterning our lives after His. When we walk in His footsteps, our reasoning no longer trips us up. We discover that God is indeed knowable, even today.

In Christ all the fullness of the Deity lives in bodily form,
and in Christ you have been brought to fullness.
He is the head over every power and authority.

COLOSSIANS 2:9–10

The Antidote to Fear

"If we have been accustomed to approach God with any mistrust
of the kindness of His feelings toward us; if our religious life
has been poisoned by fear; if unworthy thoughts of His character
and will have filled our hearts with suspicions of His goodness;
if we have pictured Him as a self-seeking tyrant; if, in short,
we have imagined Him in any way other than that which has been
revealed to us in 'the face of Jesus Christ' (2 Corinthians 4:6),
we must go back to the records of that lovely life lived among men and
must bring our conceptions of God into line with His character and ways."

If, as the scriptures tell us, Jesus is the exact representation
of God, then His qualities must mirror God's qualities. But
very often, a person's understanding of God's character is
based on childhood influences or cultural impressions that can
be misleading, deceptive, or simply wrong. Children who are
taught that God is prone to anger and punishes people at the
first sign of disobedience may well become adults who fear the
wrath of God to such an extent that they also fear approaching
Him with their needs. Fear defines their relationship with God.

But who among them fears Jesus? The person of Jesus is
not known for instilling fear, either in His followers or in those
who simply know of Him but have yet to begin following in

His footsteps. The nearly universal image of Jesus is one of tenderness and kindness, accompanied by wisdom and strength of character. He is often portrayed with open arms, welcoming children and adults alike into His presence.

If Jesus is indeed the mirror image of God, how does the perception of God as an irate tyrant line up with what the historical record says about Jesus? Was Jesus ever angry? Well, yes, He was, but only toward those who made a mockery of God by desecrating the temple and displaying religious arrogance. Everyone else is not only on safe ground, but they also have a standing invitation to join Him in a life of hope, faith, love, forgiveness, and so much more.

Seeing Jesus as a reflection of God is the perfect antidote to the poison of fear. We need never be afraid of approaching God and entering into His presence.

The Son is the image of the invisible God,
the firstborn over all creation.

COLOSSIANS 1:15

"As we look at the life of Christ and listen to His words,
we can hear God saying, 'I am rest for the weary;
I am peace for the storm-tossed; I am strength for the strengthless;
I am wisdom for the foolish; I am righteousness for the sinful;
I am all that the neediest soul on earth can want;
I am exceedingly abundantly beyond all you can ask or think.' "

On the domed ceiling of the Sistine Chapel in Vatican
City, Michelangelo created an incomparable masterpiece—
The Creation of Adam, a painting depicting God and Adam
extending their arms toward each other, their index fingers
nearly touching. It's a powerful expression of God—portrayed
as an older, white-haired man with an athletic build—reaching
out to Adam, the primary symbol of all humanity.

As profound as that image is, it does not come close to
revealing the reality of who God is. And yet, some people
continue to allow this painting and similar portrayals of God
to limit their understanding of our heavenly Father. Simply
put, any artistic rendering of a deity whose likeness can only
be imagined falls far short, because it's a product of the human
mind. Likewise, seeing God as a kindly, generous grandfather;
an exacting, stern judge; or an ethereal, angelic being hardly

does justice to the Creator and Sustainer of the universe. He is not simply a more powerful version of the beings He created.

God is "exceedingly abundantly" beyond the limitations of humanity's imagination. No one can accurately depict His being, just as nothing you can ask for surpasses His power to provide. Rest, peace, strength, wisdom, and love—and everything else that can be described as pure and good—are contained within Him. To see God is to see perfection.

We struggle with our image of God precisely because we want, and need, a visual image of perfection to set our sights on. We look around and feel as if we see only imperfection: crime, poverty, illness, tragedy. Goodness exists as well, but we want to see something that is untainted by the failings of humanity. That "something" can only be God, so our finite minds create a picture of Him—and it, too, is tainted by our humanity.

Does that mean it's wrong to try to visualize God? Not at all. We just need to realize that as we are trying to picture God, He is saying to us, "I am so much more."

In the beginning you laid the foundations of the earth,
and the heavens are the work of your hands.

PSALM 102:25

No Matter What

"You must say to yourself, 'I am going to believe what Christ says about God. No matter what my own thoughts and feelings are, nor what anybody else may say, I know that what Christ says about God must be true, for He knew, and I am going to believe Him no matter what. He says that He was one with God, so all that He was God is, and I will never be frightened of God anymore.'"

$\mathcal{W}$hen asked about the nature of faith, many people say that it is a matter of the heart. They would be right; the heart believes what the mind cannot comprehend, just as it believes what the eye cannot see. That is the very definition of faith: confidence in what is hoped for and evidence of what cannot be seen.

But faith is also a matter of the mind; it's a decision to trust God. The heart and mind must always work in tandem if faith is to survive the derision and doubts that followers of God often face. If the ridicule of others breaks your heart, it won't take much for your mind to justify giving up a life of faith. And if your mind is diverted by doubts about the faithful nature or very existence of God, your heart may tire of the battle.

But God provides His people with the strength to maintain their faith in Him whenever their hearts and minds become vulnerable to disdain and uncertainty. And one of the means He uses is the seemingly simple but powerful ability of the mind to make an unwavering decision to believe what God says about Himself rather than what others say about Him.

Some people mock God's followers for their "childish" belief in what they see as a figment of their imagination. No matter; His people know He exists and He is worthy of their faith. Others argue that God is a bloodthirsty, wrathful bully who delighted in the death of a delusional man who claimed to be His Son. But the people of God know better, because they believe that a sane man, God's Son, showed them a Father who is compassionate, loving, and forgiving to the point of sacrifice.

The moment we decide to believe the truth about God is a moment of unparalleled fortification of our faith. It's a "no matter what" moment—no matter what happens, we choose to trust the only one who is trustworthy.

Happy are those who make the LORD their trust,
who do not turn to the proud, to those who go astray after false gods.

PSALM 40:4 NRSV

"Among all the names that reveal God, the 'God of all comfort' seems to me one of the loveliest and most absolutely comforting. The words 'all comfort' speak of no limitation and no deductions. One would suppose that, however full of discomforts the outward life of the followers of such a God might be, their inward life must be a comfortable life."

As she neared the end of her life, an elderly cancer patient found little relief from the pain that plagued her, despite the best efforts of the hospice workers caring for her. Her obvious suffering was taking its toll on her caregivers, whose mission was to make the terminally ill as comfortable as possible for whatever time they had left on earth. After one volunteer noticed the books in her room that she had once enjoyed, he took it upon himself to read to her for a few minutes every morning and afternoon, even though she was seldom able to respond to him or acknowledge his presence.

One day the volunteer brought a small volume of poetry from his own limited library. One poem in particular, he told his semiconscious patient, had brought his wife great comfort during her own terminal illness. As expected, his patient did not respond. Undeterred, he began reading the poem aloud. It spoke of the comfort of God's presence as the author grieved over the death of her husband.

The volunteer suddenly sensed a subtle but unusual alertness in his patient. Her eyes were still closed, but she managed to smile as a few teardrops fell to her pillow. She even chuckled softly.

"My husband. . .my poem," she whispered before she slipped back into her sleep-like state.

The volunteer looked for the author's name on the cover. But it was not there, something he hadn't noticed before. On the flyleaf, though, was a brief mention of the apparently publicity-shy writer—and her name was the same as that of the hospice patient.

When God provides comfort to us, He wants us to share it, just as the poet's writing comforted the volunteer who had become her caregiver. He, in turn, gave back to her the very words of comfort that she had written. As we face inevitable turbulence in our outward lives, we often sense God calming our inward lives. So contagious is God's comfort that when we see storms in the lives of others, we find ourselves sharing it— sometimes in surprising and unexpected ways.

Blessed be the God and Father of our Lord Jesus Christ, the Father of mercies and God of all comfort, who comforts us in all our tribulation, that we may be able to comfort those who are in any trouble, with the comfort with which we ourselves are comforted by God.

2 CORINTHIANS 1:3–4 NKJV

A Living Epistle

*"It is easy enough to say many beautiful things about
God being the God of all comfort, but unless we know what it is to be
really and truly comforted ourselves, we might as well talk to the wind.
People must read in our lives what they hear in our words,
or all our preaching is worse than useless."*

A high school senior had dated an older boy for less than
a month in 1966 when he was ordered to report to an army
recruiting office. With a 1-A draft status, he knew he would
probably end up in Southeast Asia. But the two never talked
about that during those first few weeks of dating.

His girlfriend was unaware of how he felt about her. For
years he had watched her from a distance, sensing that they
were a matching set. When he felt she was attracted to him as
well, he asked her out. Occasional phone conversations during
the week eased the time between their weekly dates.

His letters started coming soon after he arrived in boot
camp and continued during his three-year enlistment, which
included two tours in Vietnam. Soon he professed his love for
her. Would she consider waiting for him if he returned alive?
He knew he was asking a lot; she was young, and committing
to a soldier always carried the chance that she would never

see him again. Several of their high school friends had not survived the conflict.

She wondered if he was just homesick. Was he romanticizing their brief relationship? She wasn't sure, but she took the chance.

Forty years, three children, and five grandchildren later, she was glad she did. He had returned from Vietnam and proved himself to be a "living epistle"—living proof that his character aligned with the words of comfort he had written during the bleakest time in his life. His compassion and love for her had come to life.

The words we speak can provide immeasurable comfort to others. But words sometimes fail us. We grope for the right words to say when an acquaintance has experienced devastating loss. That's when we have the opportunity to become the "living epistles" that the apostle Paul wrote about. When we have compassion for others, our presence can provide the comfort that gives substance to the words that seem so inadequate.

You yourselves are our letter, written on our hearts, known and read by everyone. You show that you are a letter from Christ, the result of our ministry, written not with ink but with the Spirit of the living God, not on tablets of stone but on tablets of human hearts.

2 CORINTHIANS 3:2–3

Ordinary Moments

"Comfort, whether human or divine, is pure and simple comfort, nothing else. None of us care for pious phrases, we want realities; and the reality of being comforted and comfortable seems to me almost more delightful than any other thing in life. We all know what it is. When as little children we cuddled up in our mother's lap after a fall and felt her loving arms around us, we had comfort. When, as grown-ups, after a hard day's work, we have put on our slippers and seated ourselves by the fire, in an easy chair with a book, we have had comfort. When, after a painful illness, we have begun to recover and have been able to stretch our limbs and open our eyes without pain, we have had comfort. . . . We cannot fail, therefore, to understand the meaning of this name of God, the 'God of all comfort.' "

$\mathcal{H}$annah Whitall Smith gave her book the title *The God of All Comfort* with great intention. She understood "all" comfort to mean rest and relief in every area of life, not only in those moments of profound sorrow but also when God's comfort permeates the ordinary moments as well.

An aging but still active woman wakes up to yet another new pain, another bout with stiffness in her knees that signals the inevitable end to her jogging days. A social worker wonders yet again if he made the right call in returning a child to his mother even though there was no evidence of her alleged abuse. A high school sophomore tries—unsuccessfully—to dismiss her classmates' relentless teasing about her weight.

Where will these people turn for comfort? What if they don't know they can turn to God? Those who have developed the habit of turning to God throughout the day realize just how much He cares about the myriad sources of our distress. Physical pain, doubt, humiliation, fatigue, loneliness—those factors and many more contribute to our restlessness and discomfort with life. We need relief, and God knows it.

God doesn't just appear on the scene in times of crisis. He actively works in our lives all the time, around the clock. That means His comforting presence is at hand when our feet ache or the neighbors' music is giving us fits or the laptop is overheating once again. He is the God of all comfort, providing the relief we need—no matter the cause of our discomfort.

Even though I walk through the valley of the shadow of death,
I fear no evil, for You are with me;
Your rod and Your staff, they comfort me.

PSALM 23:4 NASB

"I am happy to say that that stern judge is not there. He does not exist.
The God who does exist is a God who is like a mother.
Over and over again He declares this. 'I, even I, am He who comforts you'
(Isaiah 51:12), He says to the frightened children of Israel.
And then He reproaches them for not being comforted.
'Why,' He says, 'should you let anything make you afraid
when here is the Lord, your Maker, ready and longing to comfort you?
You have feared the fury of the oppressor and have forgotten Me.
Where is the fury of the oppressor when I am nearby?' "

The image of God as a harsh judge is among the saddest misperceptions of our culture. It's an image that often stems from misreading the Old Testament, but what is especially surprising is its prevalence in a society that is largely biblically illiterate. If so many people in the West fail to read the Bible, as numerous polls indicate, then where does this idea of a stern and unmerciful God come from?

Unfortunately, it sometimes comes from God's people, though many Christians would be surprised to hear that. We may think we're doing a pretty good job of representing a loving, gracious God through our nice, polite behavior, but that may be one of the problems. We set such impossibly high standards for what it means to be a Christian that when we fail to live up to those standards, we feel we have failed God—and punishment is sure to follow. After all, when our own earthly children disobey us, we punish them—right? Little do we realize the impact our words and actions have on the world around us when we feel we have disappointed God.

The world is watching us. Will we show them a ruthless, vengeful deity who strikes out against us for the slightest infraction of His commandments and principles? Or will we show the world a Father who understands how we suffer from our own failings? Our perceptions, or misperceptions, about God's character will determine how we respond. Do we see Him as our ultimate critic or as the Bible describes God—a mother who comforts her children when they are disobedient and frightened? That choice is ours, but the truth remains—the God who comforts us is the God the world desperately needs to see.

> *[Thus says the LORD]: As a mother comforts her child,*
> *so I will comfort you; you shall be comforted in Jerusalem.*
>
> ISAIAH 66:13 NRSV

For the Whole World

"The God who exists is the God and the Father of our Lord Jesus Christ, the God who so loved the world that He sent His Son, not to judge the world, but to save it. He is the God who anointed the Lord Jesus Christ to bind up the brokenhearted, to proclaim liberty to the captives and the opening of the prison to those who are bound, and to comfort all who mourn. Please notice that all. Not a few select people, but all. Every captive of sin, every prisoner in infirmity, every mourning heart throughout the whole world must be included in this 'all.' "

Sometimes we become so focused on God's activity within our circle of like-minded people that we fail to recognize that He is available to everyone on earth today and everyone who ever lived. It's easy to develop tunnel vision that is limited by our address and our sphere of friends, and while we may be aware of the wide world "out there," it's about all we can do to keep track of our own lives.

But our narrow focus means that we run the risk of seeing others as being so markedly different from us that we fall short when it comes to truly understanding and having compassion on people of other faiths and cultures. Regardless of where they live or how they perceive God, a Sudanese mother who loses a child to malaria, a Russian alcoholic who only knows the warmth that comes from a bottle, or a Chinese student who is shamed by his addiction to pornography—all can find freedom from their suffering by turning to God.

God provided that freedom in the person of Jesus Christ, who, contrary to popular belief, did not come to earth to encourage all the good people to get together on Sunday mornings to worship Him. No, He came to set everyone free, to empower *this* young man to overcome a life of poverty, *that* single mother to find hope for her children's future, and *those* senior citizens to escape their abusive caregivers. God's comfort reverberates around the world, touching the lives of countless people who may never have heard of Jesus.

Instead of thinking of God as belonging only to an exclusive group of people who share a system of beliefs, we should rejoice that He is the God of all. His accessibility to every person is cause for great joy, because that means He is and will always be accessible to us.

God so loved the world that he gave his one and only Son,
that whoever believes in him shall not perish but have eternal life.

JOHN 3:16

Compassion, not Condemnation

"The 'God of all comfort' sent His Son to be the comforter of a mourning world. And all through His life on earth He fulfilled His divine mission. When His disciples asked Him to call down fire from heaven to consume some people who refused to receive Him, He rebuked them and said: 'You do not know what manner of spirit you are of. For the Son of man did not come to destroy men's lives but to save them' (Luke 9:55–56). He received sinners and ate with them. He welcomed Mary Magdalene when all men turned from her. He refused even to condemn the woman who was taken in the very act of sin. Always and everywhere He was on the side of sinners. That was what He was for. He came to save sinners. He had no other mission."

A few years ago a celebrated pastor, radio host, and author became well-known for calling down God's judgment on those who disobey the Ten Commandments, demanding that God inflict specific forms of punishment on the disobedient, such as wiping out whole groups of people with fires, floods, and similar natural disasters. Though colleagues tried to get him to tone down his venomous speech, he would not budge.

Then, the unthinkable happened. His son died of a drug overdose. The memory of every time he condemned "druggies" flooded the pastor's mind. Unable to handle his son's death, he took a sabbatical and retreated to an isolated cabin to deal with his grief—and his shame.

Being alone with God made him realize that the problem lay not with his failure to control his son but with his theology. Sobbing, he cried out to God. "Lord, I thought I was doing Your will! But now. . .now I don't think I know You *or* Your will!"

In an instant, his tears dried. He opened his eyes and looked around the room. He felt lighthearted. The peace of God had gently fallen on him, replacing his shame with God's love and compassion.

When we condemn others for living in a way that is contrary to God's way, we prove ourselves to be the contrary ones. Our behavior is the polar opposite of the way Jesus lived. He didn't condemn the downtrodden but allowed God to transform them. Jesus' mission was transforming lives. Can we want anything less than to see that happen in the lives of others?

God did not send his Son into the world to condemn the world,
but to save the world through him.
Whoever believes in him is not condemned.

JOHN 3:17–18

The Need for Comfort

"We may find ourselves in a 'wilderness' of disappointment and suffering, and we wonder why the God who loves us should have allowed it. But He knows that it is only in that very wilderness that we can hear and receive the 'comfortable words' He has to pour out on us. We must feel the need for comfort before we can listen to the words of comfort. And God knows that it is infinitely better for us to need His comforts and receive them than it could ever be to not need them and so be without them."

Why is there so much suffering in the world? People of all faiths and no faith ask that question. In societies where belief in God is evident, that question is often followed by another one: How can a good God allow so much suffering? Although theologians, the clergy, and the laity have offered countless theories in response to those two questions, the ultimate answers—God's answers—continue to elude humanity.

One question we can answer with certainty is this: How can people find relief from their suffering? The answer should be obvious: we find the salve for our pain and suffering in God. And while God can offer His comfort even to those who don't know Him and don't know they can call on Him, those who do know Him aren't always so quick to call on Him for help, opting instead to question His love when they find themselves in difficult circumstances.

A spiritual wilderness experience is one where we find ourselves lost in a bewildering environment, seemingly without a compass—God's guidance—to help us find our way. Such an experience can follow a traumatic incident, but not always. The stresses of everyday life can lead us straight into the wilderness as well.

What we discover in the wilderness depends in part on our openness to God. Asking Him the hard questions—"Why did You do this to me? How can I ever again believe You love me? Why have You placed me in this hellish situation?"—is a sure sign of that openness. It shows we still need God. Then, when we accept and embrace the comfort He is certain to provide, we understand, and may even appreciate, the wilderness as a place where we learn deeper truths about who God is.

My comfort in my suffering is this:
Your promise preserves my life.

PSALM 119:50

The Miracle Cure

"The psalmist tells us that God will 'comfort us on every side'
(see Psalm 71:21), and what an all-embracing comfort this is.
'On every side,' no aching spot left uncomforted. And yet, in times of
special trial, how many Christians secretly read this as though it said,
'God will comfort us on every side except just the side where our trials lie;
on that side there is no comfort anywhere'? But God says every side."

*A*nyone who has ever had the flu—and who hasn't?—is
unfortunately familiar with its myriad symptoms: chills and
fever, aches and pains, congestion and sore throat, nausea
and fatigue, or any combination of those ailments. Those
who suffer from the flu are also familiar with the diverse
medications that may or may not alleviate their discomfort.
There's no single medication that makes every symptom
disappear.

A middle-aged woman was the victim of a different multi-
symptom disorder—divorce. Her symptoms? Heartache,
betrayal, bewilderment, fear, and shattered hopes and dreams.
She longed for a magic pill that would permanently erase the
pain and the chafing memories, and would promise a bright,
financially secure future for her and her children. Without such
a miracle cure, she could not imagine facing the long years

that stretched out ahead of her. But where could she find that miracle cure?

There's obviously no magic pill she can take to ease her despair. Neither is there a medication we can take to alleviate every form of distress we encounter. But we can experience a cure that is nothing short of a miracle—the comforting presence of God Himself, who promises to ease our suffering. And yet we compartmentalize the symptoms of our distress, believing that maybe God can provide for us financially, but there's just no way we'll ever recover from the betrayal that has ruined our lives forever—God or no God.

Failing to trust God to ease our suffering only intensifies the pain. We can be our own worst enemies at times, even when we know better than to follow the course we're on. In those times, we need to remember to turn to God and trust Him for the miracle cure that only He can provide. Never forget that He is the Great Physician—and He wants to see us healed.

May your unfailing love be my comfort, according to your promise to your servant. Let your compassion come to me that I may live, for your law is my delight.

PSALM 119:76–77

Gentle Shepherd, Almighty Lord

"Repeat these familiar words to yourselves: 'The Lord is my shepherd, I shall not want.' Who is it that is your shepherd? The Lord! What a wonderful announcement! The Lord God of heaven and earth, the almighty Creator of all things, who holds the universe in His hand, He is your Shepherd and has charged Himself with the care and keeping of you as a shepherd is charged with the care and keeping of his sheep."

In our largely urban/suburban culture, most of us are out of touch with rural living and the ranches that dot the landscape. We tend to know animals as pets rather than as livestock. Watching a rancher at work is a fascinating experience, but watching a sheepherder at work is utterly eye-opening.

Gentleness characterizes the work of a good shepherd. And the reason is clear—the sheep need to be treated gently. Speaking harshly or inflicting pain simply doesn't work on sheep. If you observe the behavior of sheep, the reasons the Bible compares people to sheep are evident. Even though we often gravitate toward the herd—our peer group—and go wherever they go, we do tend to wander off and try to go our own way. That's not always a bad thing among humans—except when we get lost and, like sheep, lose sight of the shepherd, who cares for us far more than we realize.

In a familiar, classic illustration, Jesus is depicted as a shepherd carrying a sheep across His shoulders. The sheep had gone astray, and the Good Shepherd went after it, found it, and brought it back to safety. The message is obvious. When we stray too far from His presence, Jesus, our ultimate caregiver, will come after us, find us, and keep us with Him. He will do so with gentle words and a loving touch.

But the image of Jesus as the Good Shepherd is even more astonishing because He is also God, the Creator of the universe—the Almighty, the Lord, the Eternal One! We can't help but fall to our knees when we realize that our caregiver, the one who has taken on the responsibility of meeting all our needs, is also the Master of all that has ever existed and will ever exist. The one who keeps the planets and galaxies on their course is the same one who takes care of us as a shepherd cares for his sheep. It's astonishing, indeed.

O come, let us worship and bow down, let us kneel before the LORD,
our Maker! For he is our God, and we are the people
of his pasture, and the sheep of his hand.

PSALM 95:6–7 NRSV

Believing in the Shepherd

"You have said, I know, hundreds of times, 'The Lord is my shepherd,' but have you ever really believed it to be an actual fact? Have you felt safe and happy and free from care, as a sheep must feel when under the care of a good shepherd, or have you felt like a poor forlorn sheep without a shepherd, or a sheep with an unfaithful, inefficient shepherd who doesn't supply your needs and leaves you in times of danger and darkness?"

$\mathcal{L}$osing sight of the shepherd has serious consequences for the sheep. Not only are sheep unable to provide for themselves, particularly in a harsh environment, they are also unable to protect themselves from the predators that are lying in wait. We human "sheep" could learn a lot from these animals—always stay in the presence of the Shepherd.

There's more, though. Being in the presence of God doesn't necessarily mean that we have opened ourselves up to an awareness of the depth and breadth of His care for us. Knowing God is with us is not the same as recognizing and acknowledging that He is actively involved in our lives. When we come to understand that He not only provides for us but also protects us, then we have experienced Him as the Shepherd He claims to be.

His provision and protection extend beyond the physical

realm. Yes, He is faithful to meet our needs for food, clothing, shelter, and protection. But He provides so much more—courage in the midst of great challenges, joy despite sorrowful occasions, freedom from worry during anxious times, hope amid desperate situations. All of that is available to us all the time, and yet we so often allow circumstances to blind us to the abundance of help He offers.

If we could see the sacrifices a good sheepherder makes for his sheep—the long, hot days of leading the flock to rich pastureland and cool, refreshing streams, the equally long but cold nights listening for nocturnal predators—we would only catch a glimpse of the way the Good Shepherd cares for us. He gave His very life as a sacrifice for each and every one of us. That alone should make us sing His praises throughout the day as He provides for us and through the night as He watches over us.

You were like sheep going astray, but now you have returned
to the Shepherd and Overseer of your souls.

1 Peter 2:25

Trusting the Good Shepherd

"But here, perhaps, you will meet me with the words,
'Oh, no, I don't blame the Lord, but I am so weak and foolish and
ignorant that I am not worthy of His care.' But don't you know that sheep
are always weak and helpless and silly, and that the very reason a shepherd
cares for them is because they are so unable to take care of themselves?
Their welfare and their safety do not in the least depend upon
their own strength or their wisdom or on anything in themselves,
but completely on the care of their shepherd. And if you are a sheep,
you also must depend completely on your Shepherd."

When we trust God to take care of us in both the good times and the difficult times, we can be assured that our lives will reflect that care. Think again about those dependent and defenseless sheep. Without a shepherd to lead them to lush meadows and clear streams, and keep hungry wolves at bay, the flock would be a sorry lot indeed. Those that managed to escape the sharp teeth and strong jaws of predators would still have to fend for themselves when it came to sheer survival. But unlike sheep we're capable of defending ourselves—more capable than sheep, anyway—and we certainly know how to keep ourselves well fed and hydrated in order to stay alive, right?

But that attitude of self-sufficiency is exactly what can get us in trouble. We are entirely at fault for the sorry lot we've become. We certainly can't blame the Good Shepherd. He willingly offered Himself as our caregiver, promising to meet all our needs and proving Himself worthy of our trust by fulfilling that promise.

Why do we attempt on our own to keep the "wolves" at bay—those people or habits or influences that threaten to devour us? Why are we so determined to work night and day to acquire possessions we don't need? In this regard, sheep have the advantage. They know that the condition of their lives— their health and their very survival—depends on the goodness of their caregiver, the Good Shepherd.

Ours does, too. The goodness of our caregiver is what keeps us spiritually alive and kicking—kicking against all the things that try to deter us by robbing us of our joy and our faith. But Satan's attacks can't get past our caregiver—the Good Shepherd.

May the God of peace, who through the blood of the eternal covenant brought back from the dead our Lord Jesus, that great Shepherd of the sheep, equip you with everything good for doing his will.

HEBREWS 13:20–21

*"If an owner of sheep is thinking of employing a shepherd,
he requires a reference from the shepherd's last employer, that he
might learn from him how his flock fared under this shepherd's care.
Now, the Lord makes statements about Himself as a good Shepherd. He
is telling the universe, the world, and the Church, 'I am the good shepherd.'
And if they ask, 'Where are Your sheep, what condition are they in?'
can He point to us as being a credit to His care? And is it not grievous if
any of us refuse to let the Shepherd take care of us, and so bring discredit
to His name by our sad condition? The universe is watching to see what
the Lord Jesus Christ is able to make of us, and what kind of sheep
we are, whether we are well fed, healthy, and happy. Their verdict
concerning Him will largely depend upon what they see in us."*

After investigating a mistaken report of a grass fire in a rural area of a western state, a sheriff's deputy saw what appeared to be a herd of horses in a pasture parched by a decade-long drought. The deputy pulled out his binoculars for a closer look, finding it hard to believe that anyone would expect their horses to find nourishment in those dried-up grasses.

What he saw sickened him—nearly a dozen emaciated horses and the rotting corpses of three others. These were not the wild horses found in some parts of the West; they belonged to someone who had no concern for their well-being. The resulting investigation revealed that the couple who owned the horses also owned half a dozen other animals, some pets, in a similar state of neglect. They were arrested and charged with animal cruelty.

Imagine how foolish it would be to blame the animals for the condition they were found in. The responsibility lay squarely on the shoulders of their owners. Likewise our lives reflect on our God. Would God, as our caretaker, turn us away after assuring us we were in His loving care? Absolutely not. But when we turn away from Him and end up spiritually emaciated, the people around us, knowing we profess to love and trust God, have to wonder just what kind of God we serve. Our vibrant, joyful lives offer the answer that our God is a loving, watchful caretaker.

My sheep listen to my voice; I know them, and they follow me.
I give them eternal life, and they shall never perish;
no one will snatch them out of my hand.

JOHN 10:27–28

Intentional Misery

"Well may we be lost in amazement at the thought that God has purposed such a glorious destiny for His sheep as to make known to the universe His 'manifold wisdom' by what He has done for us! Surely this should make us eager to abandon ourselves to Him in the most generous trust for salvation, that He may get great glory in the universe and the whole world may be won to trust Him. But if we will not let Him save us, if we reject His care and refuse to feed in His pastures or lie down in His fold, then we shall be a starved and shivering flock, sick and full of complaints, bringing dishonor on Him and hindering the world from coming to Him."

When a sheep wanders away from its master, we can be fairly certain some influence is at work. Maybe the sheep was distracted by something it saw or heard and just had to follow it, or possibly it was separated from the flock because an injury slowed it down. Sheep—being highly dependent on their shepherd for sustenance and survival—are unlikely to leave the care of the master out of anger or pride.

That's one of the many things that separate sheep behavior from human behavior. The expression "biting the hand that feeds you" reflects the unfortunate but not unusual human act of turning on someone who has provided for us and treated us well. It's bad enough when we do that to people—our parents or someone who has been generous to us—but it's especially egregious when we turn on our Shepherd, the one who has cared for us in unimaginable ways and has given us much more than we deserve.

Whenever we reject God, we intentionally embrace the misery of the wilderness, a place far from the abundance of God's provision and the comfort of His presence. Those who stay within the fold but refuse to give themselves completely to His care experience diminished, default lives that fall far short of the abundant life God promised us.

We need to see our refusal to follow God for the supremely arrogant and foolish act that it is. Do we believe we can care for ourselves better than God does? If our answer is a resounding "No!" then we can safely count ourselves among the sheep in His flock.

I will make [my people] and the region around my hill
a blessing; and I will send down the showers in their season;
they shall be showers of blessing . . . You are my sheep,
the sheep of my pasture and I am your God, says the Lord God.

EZEKIEL 34:26, 31 NRSV

Whose Shepherd Is He?

"Say the words over to yourself with all the willpower you can muster,
'The Lord is my Shepherd. He is. No matter what I feel,
He says He is, and He is. I am going to believe it, come what may.'
Then repeat the words with a different emphasis each time:
'The Lord is my Shepherd. The Lord is my Shepherd.
The Lord is my Shepherd. The Lord is my Shepherd.'"

The opening line of Psalm 23—"The Lord is my shepherd"—rings with a truth so familiar that it's easy to miss the profound impact of its words. Many who grew up in the church associate the verse with countless Sunday school lessons and posters and coloring pages. Even those who have no church background have heard those words spoken at funeral services; the psalm is a natural choice for such occasions since it expresses God's comfort in a time of loss.

"The Lord is my shepherd." On the surface it's a clear statement, but it's time for us to take a deeper, longer look at those words, one by one, starting with the word *Lord*. Could it be that we've heard and said that word so often that it's lost its meaning in our lives? Lord is not just a title; it also represents God's relationship to us. If He is truly our Lord, then He must be our Master as well, the one we obey. That's a tough concept to convey to a culture that values independence, but those who know God as their Lord understand that dependence on God trumps stubborn self-reliance every time.

The word *is* seems so inconsequential that we're tempted to skip right over it. But because the verb is present tense, it represents a state of being *now*. The Lord wasn't our Shepherd only when Psalm 23 was written, and He will not only be our Shepherd when we are in His presence after we die. God is our eternal Shepherd—past, present, and future. He exists outside of our time constraints and always *is*. Including right now.

If we ignore the word *my*, then we fail to embrace the personal nature of our relationship to the Shepherd. *My* speaks of a special relationship; Jesus is not just the Shepherd of that flock over there—He is my Shepherd! Mine!

Who is He? He is our Shepherd, our caretaker, caregiver, provider, protector. He is our Lord.

The Lord is my shepherd, I lack nothing.

PSALM 23:1

Just Like Sheep

"Lose sight of yourself for a moment and try to put yourself in the Shepherd's place. Consider your condition as He considers it. See Him coming out to seek you in your far-off wandering. See His tender, yearning love, His longing to save you. Believe His own description of Himself, and take Him at His own sweet word. Begin to trust and follow your Shepherd now and here. Abandon yourself to His care and guidance and trust Him utterly."

$\mathcal{I}$f we want to understand God as our Shepherd, it helps to learn whatever we can about the sheep. Even though their fleece looks white and soft and fluffy from a distance, in real life, sheep don't paint such a pretty picture.

The first thing people usually notice when they see sheep up close is how dirty they can be. Sheep don't like to be cleaned or to have their fleece shorn. They're stubborn, helpless, vulnerable, panicky, and susceptible to herd mentality, among other things. All in all, they can be challenging to raise and require more care than any other livestock.

Despite all that, a good sheepherder works relentlessly to keep his flock safe and healthy, even when the sheep try to go their own way and risk wandering into territory replete with poisonous plants (which they will eat), foul water (which they will drink), and hungry predators (which they can seldom outrun). Like a caring parent, the shepherd continues to take care of his flock even when the sheep in his charge seem oblivious to the fact that they are dependent on his goodness and his sacrifices on their behalf.

If we could experience the life of a shepherd for just one day, we would have a newfound appreciation for God's role as our Shepherd. Most of us can't shadow a shepherd, but we can try to imagine ourselves as a shepherd of people. How many of us would take care of a bunch of willful, fearful, and filthy people who also stink, day after day? And how would we feel if we did take on that responsibility and the people defied us at every turn?

We honor the Shepherd and show our gratitude for His care whenever we obey Him and take Him at His word. He has promised to care for us; we can return the favor by aligning our lives with that promise.

He will feed his flock like a shepherd; he will gather the lambs in his arms, and carry them in his bosom, and gently lead the mother sheep.

ISAIAH 40:11 NRSV

Green Pastures Await Us

"Thousands can testify that when they have put themselves absolutely into His hands, He has quieted the raging tempest and has turned their deserts into blossoming gardens. I don't mean that there will be no more outward trouble or care or suffering, but these very places will become green pastures and still waters inwardly to the soul. The Shepherd knows what pastures are best for His sheep. Perhaps He sees that the best pastures for some of us are to be found in the midst of opposition or earthly trials. If He leads you there, you may be sure they are green pastures for you and that you will grow to be made strong by feeding in them."

Some years ago a business owner in a small New Jersey town was facing what seemed to be an endless stream of problems. The local economy was in a free fall, and his clothing factory was losing business to cheaper manufacturers in other countries. He had invested everything in the company, and he stood to lose it all, including his house and any hope of a college education for his children.

After spending years as a nominal Christian, he knew it was time to get serious with God. It wasn't easy; he was a self-made man who depended on no one. In a humbling moment, he laid everything out before God—his family, business, house, and possessions—and said, "I've done all I can. It's out of my hands now. I want You to take over completely." Relief swept over him. He was confident God would save the company and his family's hope for the future.

Things didn't go quite as he expected. The economy worsened, his business failed, and he sold the factory to a developer who demolished it. At first stunned by God's seeming unwillingness to save his company, the owner soon came to his spiritual senses. He realized he had been trusting in the business and not in God. God had not failed him. With or without the factory, God would take care of him and his family.

In time, he laughed at the foolishness of placing his hope and trust in a crumbling building and a dying industry. The site of the now-demolished factory became a "green pasture" for him, a place where he found a greater confidence in God's care than ever before. We all need to see our trials and difficulties in the same way, as green pastures where we can rest in God's loving care.

You will keep in perfect peace those whose minds are steadfast, because they trust in you.

ISAIAH 26:3

"If each one of you will enter into this relationship with Christ and really be a helpless, trusting sheep, believing Him to be your Shepherd, and will follow Him wherever He leads, you will soon lose all your old spiritual discomfort and know the peace of God that surpasses all understanding to keep your hearts and minds in Christ Jesus."

$\mathcal{I}$n the aftermath of tragedy, TV cameras and cell phones often capture video of the raw emotions of the survivors and the victims' loved ones. Viewers usually get what they expect to see—sobs and hugs and dazed people falling apart emotionally or doing their best to remain stoic. When tragedies strike large numbers of people, chaos and confusion are added to the mix.

Almost inevitably, a reporter will ask a weeping bystander, "Can you tell us how you feel?" causing even more tears to fall. The pain is unimaginable. Empathetic viewers feel helpless; how can they console those who have lost so much and who are in such deep emotional turmoil?

At some point—maybe right away, maybe days or weeks later—a reporter is likely to stumble upon some whose demeanor is markedly different. It could be a woman who lost her elderly mother to fire or a young man whose best friends were killed in a crash. But their bearing reflects a calmness that the reporter and her audience find hard to comprehend. Didn't they just lose their loved ones? Don't they care?

They are experiencing what the Bible calls "the peace of God, which surpasses all understanding" (Philippians 4:7 NKJV). It can't be manufactured or duplicated or imitated. It's real, and it comes from a place outside of human nature. Human nature wants to scream and cry and see someone pay for the loss. But when the peace of God descends on us, it overwhelms our base instincts. God's indescribable consolation sees us through the worst times of our lives.

Fortunately, we don't have to suffer a tragedy to experience the peace of God. When we're stressed out over a medical diagnosis, God's peace can soothe our anxiety. When we have car trouble on a dark and lonely road, God's peace can shine a light in the darkness. And when we're feeling depressed and have no idea why, God's peace can brighten our spirits. We need to understand that it's always available to us—even though we cannot fathom it.

The peace of God, which surpasses all understanding,
will guard your hearts and minds through Christ Jesus.

PHILIPPIANS 4:7 NKJV

The Ideal Father

"One of the most illuminating names of God is the one especially revealed by our Lord Jesus Christ, the name of Father. I say especially revealed by Christ, because, while God had been called throughout the ages by many other names, Christ alone has revealed Him to us under the all-inclusive name of Father—a name that holds within itself all other names of wisdom and power, of love and goodness, a name that embodies for us a perfect supply for all our needs."

One of the most powerful images of God is that of a loving Father. But it's also an image that alienates people whose fathers were less than loving, even brutal, cruel, and abusive. How can we help the children of absentee or hateful fathers reconcile their only fatherly point of reference with the image of God as Father? The truth is, we can't. There is no common ground between a bad father and the only perfect one, God Himself.

What we can do is help them—and ourselves, if we suffered at the hands of an evil father—create a new image of what a good father is like. Just imagine what the ideal father would be like, because that's what we have in God. Start with some of the more obvious traits: The ideal father would certainly be loving and protective and would provide for his family to meet their needs. Add to that attributes like being wise, gentle but strong, affectionate, patient, trustworthy, kind, generous with his time, a discerning leader, a great role model, and fun to be with. There's more, of course, but already that's a tall order. Some fathers may display those traits at times, but the only one who can be all those things all of the time and perform His role to perfection is God the Father.

Instead of limiting our heavenly Father's character to that of our earthly father, we should visualize the ideal father—and realize we already have that and much more in God our Father. Wouldn't others be better off if we helped them do the same? The choice is ours. We can think of God as one who is made in the image of our earthly fathers—or we can embrace the truth that God is the good and loving and perfect Father we have longed for.

Our Father in heaven, hallowed be your name, your kingdom come, your will be done, on earth as it is in heaven.

MATTHEW 6:9–10

God Our Mother

"God is not only a father, He is a mother as well, and we have all of us known mothers whose love and tenderness have been without bound or limit. And it is very certain that the God who created them both, and who is Himself father and mother in one, could never have created earthly fathers and mothers who were more tender and more loving than He is Himself. Therefore if we want to know what sort of a Father He is, we must heap together all the best of all the fathers and mothers we have ever known or can imagine, and we must tell ourselves that this is only a faint image of our Father in heaven."

When we start to acknowledge the feminine attributes of God, we realize they are not all that different from the male attributes. But the image does change, doesn't it? Right away we notice one concept that's missing from the list of fatherly traits—nurturing. Good fathers nurture their children, too, but there's something decidedly maternal about the word that prompts us to think of a mother first, and it has to do with the connection between nurturing and nourishment.

Until the invention of infant formula, babies were greatly dependent on their mothers for nourishment. The metaphor is striking when we think of God as our Father; it conveys our particular dependence on Him for our strength and sustenance. As we begin our relationship with Him we learn how to live with Him rather than without Him.

When children grow, they are weaned from milk and gradually given more solid food. Just as they still depend on their mothers to feed them after they are weaned, so we continue to depend on God for our spiritual growth and increased understanding of His Word. As we mature we are assured of His love and convinced that nothing can separate us from it.

Before the modern time of dual-income households and babysitters, children usually experienced their mothers' constant presence—another attribute of God. No matter where we are, what we are doing, whom we are with, God is there. In God we have the perfect parent. Although we tend to think of Him primarily as a father, we need to remember that He is a mother as well—and in that unity of gender traits we begin to glimpse an image of God that reflects how completely He meets our needs.

I have calmed and quieted myself,
I am like a weaned child with its mother; like a weaned child I am content.
Israel, put your hope in the LORD both now and forevermore.

PSALM 131:2–3

Unexpected Gifts

"Our Lord draws the comparison between earthly fathers and our heavenly Father in order to show us, not how much less good and tender and willing to bless is our heavenly Father but how much more. 'If you then, being evil,' He says, 'know how to give good gifts to your children, how much more will your Father who is in heaven give good things to those who ask Him!' (Matthew 7:11). Can we imagine a good earthly father giving a stone or a snake to a hungry child instead of bread or fish? Would not our whole souls be repulsed by a father who could do such things?"

On the American frontier in the nineteenth century, celebrating a child's birthday meant merely acknowledging the day. Gifts were not expected; most families had only the bare necessities, and parents tried not to spoil their children. When one pioneer girl woke on her tenth birthday, all she expected was additional chores. As the eldest child, she feared that entering double digits meant twice as much work.

The birthday girl's mouth watered at the aroma of the sweet potato pie her mother had made for her birthday. When everyone had finished their portion, she asked if she could have the little bit left on the pie plate. "There's something you need to do before you have more pie," her father said.

Oh no. Here it comes—another chore. Her mother handed her

a bundle wrapped in a kitchen towel. She probably had to knead the dough for the bread. That wasn't so bad; she'd been doing that for years.

As she unwrapped the towel, her eyes widened. It wasn't bread dough! It was a beautiful rag doll made from fabric scraps! She could hardly believe it. She hadn't had a doll since they had moved to Kansas a long, long time ago.

"One of your new chores will be taking care of her and sharing her with your sister. I hope that won't be too hard," her father said, his eyes shining. "And don't forget to finish the pie."

God not only loves to give us good gifts; He also loves to surprise us with them. No matter what we ask for, He always gives us so much more. Sometimes, that "much more" is as apparent as a birthday gift, but sometimes it comes in the form of His behind-the-scenes activity on our behalf—which is why we need to thank Him for all His gifts, seen and unseen.

Every good and perfect gift is from above,
coming down from the Father of the heavenly lights,
who does not change like shifting shadows.

JAMES 1:17

Have No Fear

"It is not only that our heavenly Father is willing to give us good things. He is far more than willing. Our Lord says, 'Do not fear, little flock, for it is your Father's good pleasure to give you the kingdom' (Luke 12:32). There is no grudging in His giving; it is His 'good pleasure' to give; He likes to do it. He wants to give you the kingdom far more than you want to have it. Those of us who are parents know how eager we are to give good things to our children, and this may help us to understand how it is God's 'good pleasure' to give us the kingdom. Why, then, should we ask Him with such fear, and why should we be anxious that He might fail to grant what we need?"

One of the marks of good parenting is the ability to earn a child's respect without making him or her feel fearful. Parents who instill fear may have children who appear respectful—they're too afraid to behave any other way!—but in reality, they have little respect for their parents, something that will become more and more apparent as they grow older.

Many of us have known people who appear to be submissive to God's will, but deep down, they have little love and respect for Him. Others are so afraid of Him that they try to hide by ignoring Him. Unfortunately, sometimes people learn to fear God from believers who speak carelessly about

God "punishing" someone for behavior they have judged to be wrong. The way we speak about God has consequences, for both good and bad.

So how can we be more careful to portray God as the loving, trustworthy Father He is? First we must believe it ourselves and live accordingly. If we project a sense of anxiety over our family life or our finances or any other aspect of our lives, we are telling others that our God is not the good and gracious Father we say He is.

To better understand the faithfulness of God's provision, we need only to think of the lengths to which good parents go to reduce their children's anxiety over the stresses of everyday life. And realize that our heavenly Father does so much more.

Your Father knows what you need before you ask him.

MATTHEW 6:8

Where Our Burdens Belong

" 'Behold,' says the apostle John, 'what manner of love the Father has bestowed on us, that we should be called children of God!' (1 John 3:1). The 'manner of love' bestowed on us is the love of a father for his son, a tender, protecting love that knows our weakness and our need and cares for us accordingly. He treats us as sons, and all He asks in return is that we treat Him as a Father we can trust without anxiety. We must take the son's place of dependence and trust and let Him keep the father's place of care and responsibility."

Soon after Christmas, a mother found her eight-year-old son once again counting the money he had received from several relatives. The money was to go into his savings account, and she was about to scold him for "playing" with it before they could get to the bank.

"Here." The boy handed her the pile of bills and checks. "You and Daddy can have it for the rent."

Oh no, his mother thought. *He heard us talking about our debt. Maybe he's just being generous. That's sweet. . .no need to worry.*

But two days later, she opened her e-mail account to discover messages from online employment services with information about job openings for her son, who had passed himself off as an eighteen-year-old.

As his mother talked to him that night about why he shouldn't have done what he did, he trembled and started to sob; his worry over the family's problems was having a more serious effect on him than his parents thought. As his mother held him, prayed for him, and tried to reassure him that they could handle their bills, he began to calm down and slowly drifted off to sleep.

This young child was stressed out about a problem that was not his to solve. We can see so clearly that he needed to leave the problem in his parents' hands and get back to the business of being a kid.

Why, then, are we so blind to the times we take on burdens that belong in God's hands? If we could only learn to let God carry our burdens and calm our troubled spirits. After all, we have an important job to attend to—the business of living the joyful life He planned for us all along.

Those who know your name put their trust in you, for you,
O LORD, have not forsaken those who seek you.

PSALM 9:10 NRSV

The Spirit of Adoption

"If ever an earthly father was worthy of the confidence of his children, surely much more is our heavenly Father worthy of our confidence. The remedy for our discomfort and unrest is in becoming acquainted with the Father. 'For,' says the apostle Paul, 'you did not receive the spirit of bondage again to fear, but you received the spirit of adoption by whom we cry out, "Abba, Father"'" (Romans 8:15). Is it this 'spirit of adoption' that reigns in your heart, or is it the 'spirit of bondage'? Your whole comfort in the religious life depends upon which spirit it is."

Whenever children are adopted, there is cause for celebration. The adoptive parents finally have the family they have longed for, and the children are likely to experience the love and stability that may have eluded them until then.

Experts say, however, that the transition into a new environment is more challenging for an older child than for an infant. The adopting parents *know* that this child is the one for them, but the child may not be so confident. Who are these people who want me to live with them and call them Mom and Dad? Can I trust them?

New believers also need to adjust to their new lives with God. Is He really as faithful as everyone says He is? Will He take care of me, or will I be on my own again? Who is He, anyway? The answers to those questions come with time, and the more time we spend with God, the more satisfying the answers will be. We discover soon enough that the Father who adopted us into His family is good and kind and will not beat us. With each day we spend with Him, we come to know Him better. Still, more questions always emerge: How can He be so gracious toward me? Could He really forgive me for that?

It's fine to ask those questions, because they are what lead us to the answers. A good earthly father welcomes questions from his children. God does the same—and He doesn't get exasperated by the number of times we ask the same question! The "spirit of adoption" means that we will never have any reason to be afraid of God—even if we confess our fear of Him. His comforting presence will allay all our fears.

In love he predestined us for adoption to sonship through Jesus Christ,
in accordance with his pleasure and will—
to the praise of his glorious grace.

EPHESIANS 1:4–6

The "I AM"

"Of all the names of God perhaps the most comprehensive is the name Jehovah. The word Jehovah means 'the self-existing One, the I am,' and it is generally used as a direct revelation of what God is. In several places an explanatory word is added, revealing one of His special characteristics, and it is to these that I want to particularly call attention. They are as follows:

> *"Jehovah-jireh: the Lord will see, or the Lord will provide*
> *"Jehovah-nissi: the Lord my Banner*
> *"Jehovah-shalom: the Lord our Peace*
> *"Jehovah-tsidkenu: the Lord our Righteousness*
> *"Jehovah-shammah: the Lord is there"*

Jehovah is a word not often heard today outside of churches and synagogues, but it's a word that is rich with meaning. It's not simply an Old Testament word for God; it's the most complete expression of the all-encompassing nature of God. He is the "I am"—the one who is and was and always will be. God is the universal being who exists outside of time, in infinity and eternity. Yes, Jehovah is a difficult concept to wrap our heads around. Just when we think we understand it—Him— we realize we don't.

At first glance, we may look at the various attributes the Israelites attached to the word *Jehovah* to emphasize a particular aspect of God's nature. Jehovah-jireh conveys the idea of the Lord as our provider; wouldn't it be wonderful if we had an equivalent word in English? Or Jehovah-shalom—the Lord our Peace. Well, what's stopping us? Granted, most of us don't have the influence it would take to coin a new word. But we can use equivalent English phrases in our thoughts and in our prayers:

"God my Provider, thank You for giving me everything I need and so many things I want and a lot of things I never would have thought to ask for."

"God my Righteousness, I am so grateful to You that I do not have to depend on my own feeble attempts at righteous living—that You sent Jesus to be my righteousness."

Our private time with God provides the perfect opportunity for us to be specific about the way we see the Lord working in our lives at any given moment. When He has quelled the anxiety in our hearts, addressing Him as "God my Peace" makes for a more intimate conversation as we acknowledge His recent influence on our lives. Instead of a distant, Old Testament Jehovah, we begin to see God as the "I am," the ever-present one.

That they may know that You, whose name alone is the LORD, are the Most High over all the earth.

PSALM 83:18 NKJV

God Our Provider

"Over and over our Lord urges us to take no care, because God cares for us. 'Your heavenly Father knows,' He says, 'that you need all these things' (Matthew 6:32). If the Lord sees and knows our needs, of course He will provide for them. Being our Father, He can't do anything else. As soon as a good mother sees that her child needs anything, she sets about supplying that need. She doesn't even wait for the child to ask—the sight of the need is asking enough. When God, therefore, says to us, 'I am He who sees your need,' He in reality says also, 'I am He who provides,' for He cannot see and fail to provide."

God has given mothers the ability to identify and even anticipate their children's needs. Fathers may have this gift, too, but mothers seem to have it in abundance. Any good and attentive mother knows when an infant is ready for another feeding, when a toddler needs a nap despite his objections to the contrary, and when her older children need a treat or a hug or to be left alone. Sometimes meeting those needs— like staying up all night with a sick or hurting child—is not convenient or pleasant, but sacrifice is a nonnegotiable component of good parenting.

God, as our loving Father and Mother, knows we humans are a needy lot. We may think we can get by on our own just as toddlers think they can, but one hour with a two-year-old proves that they require attentive care. Sure, we can prepare our own meals and dress ourselves and clean up after ourselves better than a toddler can, but in some areas we are such bundles of need that we often turn to other people, questionable or illegal substances, mindless entertainment, and myriad other things to find relief from the stresses of our daily lives.

But long ago, God provided for every need we have. He sent Jesus to be the fulfillment of humanity's quest for peace and contentment and relief from the soul-crushing burden of sin. God our Father and Mother saw and anticipated our need long before His Son, Jesus, made His appearance on earth. Jesus was the long-awaited provision of God.

Do we live as if our every need will be satisfied? Do we trust God to provide for us? If we can say yes to that, we must surely realize that we will never again have reason to worry.

The LORD will guide you always; he will satisfy your needs in a sun-scorched land and will strengthen your frame.

ISAIAH 58:11

Getting What We Need

"Often, in order to give us what we need, the Lord is obliged to keep from us what we want. Your heavenly Father knows what you need; you don't know. And if all your wants were gratified, it might well be that all your needs would be left unsupplied. It ought to be enough for us that our God is indeed Jehovah-jireh, the Lord who will see, and who will therefore provide."

We humans have a tough time distinguishing between our needs and our wants. We're like children who insist that they *need* to go to Disney World, except the consequences of not getting what we want can be far worse than a temper tantrum. Sometimes we even reject God.

"But we needed that house!" a mother of three young children insisted. "We're running out of space, and our sons have to share a bedroom! I just knew God would answer my prayers and let us have that house! Now we'll never find a house that big in our price range!"

Maybe they won't. And maybe that will be the best thing that ever happened to them. That mother felt they needed more room, but God knew they would just fill it up with more useless stuff. She felt her sons each needed a bedroom, especially since her daughter had her own room, but God knew that despite the usual sibling spats, those boys would forge a friendship that would survive their tight quarters. She felt they needed a larger house even if it meant a steeper mortgage, but God knew the economy was about to collapse, and she and her husband would both have their pay reduced.

What she saw as needs, God knew were merely wants. He knew the family should stay in the smaller house because they would need each other more than ever in the difficult days to come—they wouldn't be able to avoid each other or ignore the pain each one would experience.

We all need to discern the difference between our wants and our needs, even when our wants are not of a material nature. We may want to be left alone, but God knows we need companionship. Or vice versa—we may want to be around other people to avoid confronting ourselves, but God knows we need quiet time for reflection. Whenever we're unsure about our desires, we can be sure that God will clarify our needs.

With God are wisdom and strength;
he has counsel and understanding.

JOB 12:13 NRSV

Everything's under Control

"Faith is the one essential thing, without which all else is useless. And it means that we must not only hand the battle over to the Lord, but we must leave it with Him and have absolute faith that He will conquer. It is here that the fight comes in. It seems so unsafe to sit still and do nothing but trust the Lord, and the temptation to take the battle back into our own hands is often tremendous. To keep our hands off in spiritual matters is as hard for us as it is for a drowning man to keep his hands off the one who is trying to rescue him. . . . Our interference hinders His working. Spiritual forces cannot work while earthly forces are active."

*I*t's a familiar big-screen plot—the scared or angry or even well-intentioned character who insists on taking the law into his own hands. Someone has done him or a loved one wrong, and he decides that the authorities aren't doing enough to bring the perpetrator to justice. So he enters the fray, and we all know what's coming next: someone is going to get hurt, maybe fatally, and it's too late for us to warn him.

Wouldn't it be great if we could prevent ourselves from entering our real-life frays? We may even hear "Don't!" in our heads, but we often keep going, full steam ahead, right into the midst of a battle that God never meant for us to fight. Instead of helping our cause, we find ourselves powerless in the middle of the battlefield—and in God's way. It's as if we've tossed aside our most effective weapon—our faith in God—and somehow thought we could handle the situation on our own. The revelation that we can't often comes too late.

Sitting still and doing nothing can be next to impossible for some of us. We need to realize that trusting God is not the same thing as doing nothing, though. Faith does not sit back and wave a dismissive hand as if nothing really matters, because God is running the show. Our faith is activated—brought to life—when we believe that God has everything under control, because He does. Faith means cooperating with God, staying out of a situation when it's clear we should, and getting involved when He calls us into service.

Trust the LORD with all your heart,
and don't depend on your own understanding.

PROVERBS 3:5 NCV

The Victory of Weakness

"The Lord wrestles with us in order to bring us to a place of entire dependence on Him. We resist as long as we have any strength, until at last He is forced to bring us to a place of helplessness, where we are obliged to yield, and then we conquer by this very yielding. Our victory is always the victory of weakness."

In the bout for most undesirable trait, weakness would certainly be among the top contenders for the title. Call a man weak, and you've insulted his very manhood. Call a woman weak, and you've relegated her to a centuries-old stereotype. We're chided for the slightest sign of weakness and applauded for every show of strength.

Strength is certainly an admirable quality. But we get into trouble when we rely on our own strength instead of acknowledging our weakness and depending on God. Our abilities are limited, while God's power is limitless. What are we thinking when we set out to fight our battles alone? What's the matter with us? Well, we're just plain human. And we need to remember that.

In spiritual battles, we're like a featherweight who thinks he can go up against a heavyweight champion and not get clobbered. We know from the start that we're out of our depth;

still, we enter the ring even though God is saying to us, "This isn't your battle; I've got this." We might as well be facing Muhammad Ali in his prime. We don't stand a chance. Finally, when we've been beaten senseless, or maybe back to our senses, we lie on the mat, waiting to be carried off. Our only hope is that it's God who picks us up and tends to our bruised and battered spirits.

How much smarter would it be to forgo the battle altogether and let God do our fighting for us? The victory of weakness is admitting that we are not equal to our opponent, whatever that may be—temptation, anger, addiction, poverty, illness—and letting God do the heavy lifting. After all, He never has to fight outside His weight class.

> *[The Lord] said to me, "My grace is sufficient for you,*
> *for power is made perfect in weakness."*

2 CORINTHIANS 12:9 NRSV

Peace amid Turmoil

"Our idea of peace is that it must be outward before it can be inward, that all enemies must be driven away and all troubles cease. But the Lord's idea was of an interior peace that could exist in the midst of turmoil and triumph over it. The ground for this sort of peace is found in the fact that Christ has overcome the world. Only the conqueror can proclaim peace, and the people, whose battles He has fought, can do nothing but enter into it. They can neither make nor unmake it. But if they choose, they can refuse to believe in it and so fail to let it reign in their hearts. You may be afraid to believe that Christ has made peace for you, but He has done it, and all your continued warfare is worse than useless."

In inner-city Philadelphia, an elderly woman sits on the stoop outside her cramped row house, waiting for her grandson to get home from his pizza delivery job. It's nearly midnight, but the oppressive heat has brought everyone out of their homes and onto the street. Not surprisingly, nerves are on edge and tempers are flaring. Right now, she just wants to see the face of her grandson, the teenager she has cared for ever since his mother died six years earlier. His walk home from work will take him through some dangerous territory.

As she sat at the bedside of her dying daughter, this grandmother came face-to-face with the reality that she would be responsible for her grandson, despite her advanced years and flagging energy. A lifelong churchgoer, she remembered all the Bible verses and sermons she had heard about the peace of God and recalled times when she had experienced that peace.

But now things were different. She needed sustained peace, the kind of lasting, inner peace that would not disappear with every new difficulty.

"Well, God, it's get-real time," she prayed. "I'm taking hold of that peace I've heard so much about." Now, six years later, she knows that resident peace well. She sits on the stoop tonight, not because she's worried or afraid, but for the joy of seeing her grandson's face.

Can we claim to have a similar measure of peace in our circumstances? All that grandmother did was get real with God and claim possession of His peace. There's no reason we can't do the same.

Let me hear what God the LORD will speak, for he will speak peace to his people, to his faithful, to those who turn to him in their hearts.

PSALM 85:8 NRSV

Be Anxious for Nothing

"We can always enter into peace by a simple obedience to Philippians 4:6–7: 'Be anxious for nothing, but in everything by prayer and supplication, with thanksgiving, let your requests be made known to God; and the peace of God, which surpasses all understanding, will guard your hearts and minds through Christ Jesus.' The steps here are very plain, and they are only two. First, give up all anxiety; and second, hand over your cares to God. Then stand strong here; peace must come."

The personal assistant to the CEO of a midsized West Coast corporation realized one night, just before drifting off, that it was the ninth night in a row that he had taken a sleeping pill. He had been working such late hours for so long that he hadn't even considered the possibility of becoming addicted to sleep aids.

His boss was demanding, but it was a good job, even though it involved frequent travel and late nights at the office; what decent job didn't? Things were going okay with his girlfriend, who also had a stressful job. The last time they managed to get together, though—when was that, anyway?— she mentioned that he seemed to be flatlining emotionally. He didn't want to admit that she was right, but silently he agreed that he wasn't very enthusiastic about anything. But that was life in the twenty-first century: do whatever you've got to do to make it through each day.

Concerned about his insomnia and sleeping pill intake, he went to his doctor, confident that he could just get a prescription for a nonaddictive medication, and that would be that. But his doctor, who took a holistic approach within his traditional medical practice, insisted on getting to the root of the problem instead of jumping right to the pharmaceutical remedy. But the man couldn't clearly identify any one factor that was causing him distress; it was nothing in particular and everything in general. He was suffering from a contemporary disorder known as generalized anxiety.

When we experience anxiety that has a specific cause, we need to identify it and turn it over to God by name—"I give You the anxiety that my divorce is causing me." But things become trickier when we can't identify why we are anxious; the problem is just life itself. That's when we need to learn to "be anxious for nothing," which covers it all—the anxiety we can identify and that which we cannot.

> *When my anxious thoughts multiply within me,*
> *Your consolations delight my soul.*

PSALM 94:19 NASB

The Source of Righteousness

"Most of the struggles and conflicts of our Christian life come from our fights with sin and our efforts after righteousness. And I need not say how great are our failures. As long as we try to conquer sin or attain righteousness by our own efforts, we are bound to fail. But if we discover that the Lord is our righteousness, we will have the secret of victory."

$\mathcal{I}$n the wake of the latest scandal involving a public official or celebrity, we're likely to hear a seemingly heartfelt apology along with some variation of the confession, "I made a mistake." But wait. Is that really a confession? Certainly not in the theological sense of the word. A "mistake" is a minor error, like filling in the wrong circle on a standardized test. A confession involves a much more serious infraction. To use a word that has fallen out of favor for some time now, confession involves *sin.*

The public confession of having made a mistake is often followed by a promise: "I can assure my constituents or fans or spouse or whoever has been wronged that this will not happen again. I have changed. I will not let you down in the future." The cynics among us don't believe a word of that; the optimists among us hope that a team of professionals has helped the offender overcome his or her propensity for lying, cheating, or whatever the particular violation was. The wise among us, however, leave the judging to others but know that true transformation can come only from God.

Without Jesus, whose death and resurrection activated the possibility that we could be transformed, there is no way that we, by sheer willpower, can overcome the sins that threaten to destroy our lives. We can huff and puff with all our might, but we can't blow down the fortress of sin that bedevils us. Sure, we can give up certain things that we perceive as sinful, but even when we're successful at that—which often doesn't last all that long—we haven't gotten to the essence of the problem, which is Sin with a capital *S*, the root cause of all those things we're so proud of having given up.

Whenever we try to be "good" in our own strength, we are bound to fail. We just don't have it in us to do otherwise. But God in us—that's another story. He is the source of righteousness that never fails.

The mind governed by the flesh is death,
but the mind governed by the Spirit is life and peace.

ROMANS 8:6

Accepting God's Gifts

"If we need righteousness of any sort, such as patience, humility, or love, it is useless for us to look within, hoping to find a supply there, for we never will find it; but we must simply take it by faith, as a possession that is stored up for us in Christ, who is our righteousness. I have seen sweetness and gentleness poured like a flood of sunshine into dark and bitter spirits when the hand of faith has been reached out to grasp them as a present possession. I have seen sharp tongues made tender, anxious hearts made calm, and fretful spirits made quiet by the simple step of taking by faith the righteousness that is ours in Christ."

God has an overflowing storehouse of gifts available to each of us. Sometimes we do have to ask for them, but at other times God lavishes them on us before we even have a chance to ask. All we ever really have to do is take possession of what is ours already.

Still, there are times when we think we can draw on our own imaginary supply to meet our needs. If we need to be more patient with someone—and we've already reached the end of our patience rope—how can we possibly think we have a reserve of patience somewhere that we can draw on? We don't, but God can give us the gift of patience. Do we need to treat people more kindly? The fact that we recognize this need is a good indication that we don't have a cupboard full of excess kindness we can pull from. But we can count on God to create in us a kind heart that will pass His kindness along to others.

We would be foolish not to accept the gifts of righteousness He offers us. But refusing to reach out and take possession of them is like running out of gas but refusing to accept fuel offered by a helpful motorist, insisting instead that we have a gallon or two somewhere in the car.

There's no question that it takes faith to accept God's gift of righteousness. We may be afraid that somehow it won't "take," and we'll go back to being the same miserable, impatient, unkind person we want so desperately not to be. That fear is dispelled when we rest in His righteousness rather than our own.

God made him who had no sin to be sin for us,
so that in him we might become the righteousness of God.

2 CORINTHIANS 5:21

One Constant Presence

"Wherever the Lord is, all must go right for His children. Where the good mother is, all goes right, up to the measure of her ability, for her children. And how much more with God. His presence is enough. We can all remember how the simple presence of our mothers was enough for us when we were children. All that we needed of comfort, rest, and deliverance was ensured to us by the mere fact of our mother, as she sat in her usual chair with her work or her book or her writing, and we had burst in on her with our childish woes. If we could only see that the presence of God is the same assurance of comfort, rest, and deliverance, only infinitely more so, a fountain of joy would be opened up in our lives that would drive out every remnant of discomfort and distress."

$\mathcal{P}$aul Simon's song "Old Friends" is a poignant portrayal of a long-standing relationship between two people who are simply content with each other's presence. They don't need to talk as much as they did decades earlier, when they were first getting to know each other. They don't need to do much of anything, really. The important thing, the only thing that really matters, is the comfort of knowing that the other is there.

Knowing that God is there provides an even greater measure of comfort, because He will always be there. There may come a time when the faithful friend who joins us every day on the park bench won't show up. But God will always show up. We even expect the peripheral people in our lives—our favorite cashiers or servers or bank tellers—to always be where we expect them to be, but only God can assure us that His presence will always be with us. What a joy and comfort it is to know that we will always have this one constant presence—God!

Meditating on the eternal nature of God makes us more acutely aware of what a gift His presence is. Knowing that we can approach Him at any time, about anything—and that He will be there when we do—is all the assurance of His love that we should ever need.

[The Lord said], "Know that I am with you and will keep you wherever you go."

GENESIS 28:15 NRSV

The Futility of Self-Analysis

"God says, 'Look to Me and you will be saved,' but the self-analyzing soul says, 'I must look to myself if I am to have any hope of being saved. It must be by getting myself right that salvation is to come.' We see what we look at and cannot see what we look away from, and we cannot look to Jesus while we are looking at ourselves. The power for victory and endurance are to come from looking to Jesus and considering Him."

Self-analysis is about as futile as self-diagnosis. Depending on our tendency to see a cup as either half-empty or half-full, we may deduce that the chronic pain in our heads is a brain tumor when it's only an ongoing stress headache. Or we may diagnose it—and dismiss it—as a headache when it actually is a brain tumor. In the first case, we needlessly worry and fear going to a doctor to get it checked out; in the second, we see no need for a doctor, unaware that the tumor inside our skull is growing with every passing day.

Analyzing our spiritual illnesses is equally futile and risky. "Why can't I be a better person?" we wonder. "What's the matter with me, anyway?" So we look deep inside ourselves, or as deeply as we dare, and decide that we need to go to church more often and read the Bible more each day. But that's not the solution we need, because infrequent church attendance and sporadic Bible reading were never our problem; they were symptoms of a much deeper issue, one involving our hearts.

When our hearts are turned away from God, our spiritual health—and often our physical, emotional, and financial health—begins to suffer. And when our focus is turned inward, the problem intensifies, because we have nothing within ourselves that can provide a solution. It's a lose-lose situation.

Some of us try to work out a compromise; we try to keep one eye on Jesus and one on ourselves. It's impossible to look in two different directions with our physical eyes, and we deceive ourselves if we think we can accomplish that with our spiritual eyes. Our focus needs to be trained always and forever on Jesus. He is the perfect analyst, diagnostician, and healer of what ails us.

> *Look unto me, and be ye saved, all the ends of the earth:*
> *for I am God, and there is none else.*

Isaiah 45:22 KJV

Get Rid of It!

"It is of no use, then, for us to examine self and tinker with it in the hope of improving it, for the thing the Lord wants us to do with it is to get rid of it. The only safe and scriptural way is to have nothing to do with self at all, to ignore it altogether, and to fix our eyes, our thoughts, and our expectations on the Lord and on Him alone. We must substitute for the personal pronouns 'I,' 'me,' 'my' the pronouns 'He,' 'Him,' 'His'; and must ask ourselves, not 'am I good?' but 'is He good?'"

A middle-aged shop owner had become so sick of his anger and arrogance that he found himself thinking, *I'd leave myself if I could.* Reared in a family of macho men, he had suppressed the sensitive spirit inside in order to fit in with his male relatives. But doing so had made him more and more miserable.

Things reached a boiling point one day when he stormed out of the house after swearing at his wife and kids and tore down the highway in a rage. Once he reached the shop, he sat down and covered his face with his hands. *What just happened?* he thought. He couldn't even remember what had set him off.

Over the next few weeks, he tried to change. One of his employees took notice; his own transformation had come about only when he stopped trying to "be nice" and began to count on Jesus to change his nature. After work one night, the young man felt the time had come to share his story with the shop owner. He explained how he managed to shed his old nature—and possibly put his job on the line in the process. His boss not only listened; he also asked lots of questions and allowed the young man to pray for him.

It took some time, but the shop owner rediscovered the sensitive nature he'd had as a child, as Jesus helped him peel off layer after layer of hardened conformity to his family's expectations. The shop keeper's young employee also had a hand in his transforming, answering his boss's many questions and pointing him to resources that would help strengthen his faith.

Trying to discard bad habits only gets rid of the habits. It's our nature that needs transforming—and that only happens when we stop depending on ourselves and start trusting Jesus to change us from the inside out.

You were taught, with regard to your former way of life,
to put off your old self, which is being corrupted by its deceitful desires;
to be made new in the attitude of your minds; and to put on the new self,
created to be like God in true righteousness and holiness.

EPHESIANS 4:22–24

All Tangled Up

"The psalmist says: 'My eyes are ever toward the LORD, for he shall pluck my feet out of the net' (Psalm 25:15). As long as our eyes are looking at our own feet, and the net in which they're entangled, we only get into worse tangles. But when we keep our eyes on the Lord, He plucks our feet out of the net."

*E*nmeshment—that's a great word for all of us to learn and use. It's also a condition we need to avoid. When we become enmeshed in the lives of others, trouble is sure to follow. We get all tangled up in a net God never wanted us to be ensnared by, and the more we try on our own to disentangle ourselves, the more enmeshed we become.

What does enmeshment look like in real life? It's the mother who continues to bail out her wayward son, pleading with authorities and covering for him when he's broken yet another law. The father who thinks his son-in-law should be more ambitious, so he calls his daughter constantly with job information. The grandmother who frets over the way her daughter-in-law is rearing her only grandchild and offering constant advice that she's sure would make her grandbaby both brilliant and healthy!

Enmeshment is especially destructive in families. Few

things are as harmful to a healthy parent–adult child relationship as entanglement. It's more than uninvited involvement; it's interference that threatens to drive everyone crazy, including ourselves.

When we become entangled in other people's lives, we rob them of the joy of living on their own terms, and we keep them from learning the valuable life lessons God wants them to discover. In the process, we get all churned up inside, worrying about things that are none of our business. That's right; even if it involves our own adult children, their problems become ours only when we're invited to offer our help, advice, or wisdom.

It all comes back to trust once again. Can we trust God to help our loved ones sort out their problems? Of course. Can He do a better job of it than we can? Of course. Let's get out of the way—out of the net that has ensnared us—and allow God to get on with the business of being God, without any interference from us.

Trust in him at all times, O people;
pour out your heart before him; God is a refuge for us.

PSALM 62:8 NRSV

Recognizing God

"Somehow people seem to lay aside their common sense when they come to the subject of religion and expect to see things they've deliberately kept their backs turned toward. They cry out, 'O Lord, reveal Yourself,' but instead of looking at Him they look at themselves and their own feelings, and then wonder why God hides His face from their fervent prayers. But how can they see what they don't look at? It is never God who hides His face from us, but it is always we who hide our face from Him, turning our backs to Him rather than our faces."

From the moment she heard about the love of Jesus, a store clerk was sold on God. Brought up in a home without any spiritual underpinnings, she had long believed there was more to life than what she could see. When a friend started talking to her about God, she felt like a dehydrated hiker who had just found a refreshing mountain stream.

Taking her friend's words literally, she believed that soon she would see God with her eyes. As the months passed, she berated herself for not being a "good enough" Christian. Surely that was the problem, but she was too ashamed to ask her friend why she couldn't see God.

One day on her break she went outside and silently expressed her frustration to God: "Why can't I see You? What am I doing wrong?"

She heard nothing but the usual sounds of a busy parking lot. That was typical. Not only had she never seen God; she also had never heard His voice. As she sat on the bench watching people load groceries into their cars, she heard a question in her head—not a voice, just a question: "Do you remember when you helped that little girl find her mother in the store? Do you recall the look of joy on her face and the relief in her mother's expression? You saw Me in that reunion, but you didn't recognize Me.

"And that flash flood last month that you missed by a few minutes? I was there, holding back the floodwaters, but your panic kept you from seeing Me. I am always with you, though you won't ever see Me with your physical eyes. You *will* see Me, however, with your spiritual eyes."

If we want to see God, we need to see into the realm where He is at work, the spiritual realm.

God is spirit, and his worshipers must worship in the Spirit and in truth.

JOHN 4:24

A Cheerful, Confident Faith

*"One look at Christ is worth more for salvation than a million looks at self.
Yet so mistaken are our ideas, we seem unable to avoid thinking that the
mortification that results from self-examination must have in it some
saving power, because it makes us so miserable. For we have to travel
a long way on our heavenly journey before we fully learn that there is
no saving power in misery, and that a cheerful, confident faith
is the only successful attitude for the aspiring soul."*

To look at the demeanor of some followers of Christ,
you'd think they were Hebrew slaves laboring under the
tyrannical oppression of the Egyptian pharaoh. Salvation is
serious work, they think, and we don't have enough time on
this earth to waste on fun. They may as well return to the
Middle Ages, when well-intentioned but deceived Christians
severely injured themselves as a way of experiencing Christ's
suffering and thereby proving their faithfulness and devotion
to Him.

What a sad way to spend the few short years we have
on this broken but beautiful planet! How can we even think
that the One who gave us the people we love and the people
who love us would want us to spend our lives in misery? Do
we believe that the God who gave us otters and monkeys

and kittens doesn't want us to laugh and have a spectacularly wonder-filled life?

We can be so misguided by people who care more about following the "rules"—which are often misinterpreted or manmade—than the sheer joy in the lives of those who know God. Jesus came right out and said we couldn't follow all the rules even if we tried! He told us to love God and love each other, which seems like a much better way to live. From the way the Pharisees criticized Him for hanging out with ordinary people rather than religious leaders, it sounds as if He knew how to have a good time. If it was right for the Son of God, we can safely assume it's right for us.

The people around us need to be healed of their brokenness so they can see the beauty surrounding them. They can't be healed by more brokenness, misery, and enslavement to oppressive rules. They can only be healed by God, the one who granted us the freedom to make the most of the life He has given us.

As by one man's disobedience many were made sinners, so by the obedience of one shall many be made righteous.

ROMANS 5:19 KJV

Looking Away from Ourselves

"Let us lay aside all care for ourselves and care instead for our needy brothers and sisters. Let us stop trying to do something for our own poor miserable self-life, and begin to try to do something to help the spiritual lives of others. Let us give up our hopeless efforts to find something in ourselves to delight in, and delight ourselves only in the Lord and in His service. If we will do this, the days of our misery will be ended."

Countless people have discovered an often-overlooked cure for the depression and overall malaise that afflicts them. It usually doesn't cost anything but time, and unlike medications, there are no negative side effects. It's guaranteed to bring about a sense of joy, improved health, and general well-being.

Does that sound like a miracle cure? In a way it is, because it depends on the power of God to make it work. The cure? It's serving others as a way of serving God. There is so much need in the world, in our cities and neighborhoods, that it can seem overwhelming; we wonder how our pitiful efforts can make a difference. But as the familiar adage goes, even if we only help one person, our effort has made a difference to that person.

Serving others also makes a huge difference in our lives, far beyond the payoff of feeling good about ourselves. It opens our eyes to the depth of spiritual need in the world, and that often becomes a mirror into our own spiritually needy souls. When we serve those who are not like us, we realize that while we think we are there to help them, we discover how strong, capable, and even rich they are in the things that really matter. They may help us in ways we could never have imagined.

Any time we take our eyes off ourselves is a good time! When we look to Jesus, we will often find Him pointing to the people He wants us to serve on His behalf. If we ignore Him and continue to think only about our own needs, we have no one to blame but ourselves when we end up wallowing in depression once again. When we choose to give our lives in service to others, we are finally freed from the quicksand of our own making.

Serve wholeheartedly, as if you were serving the Lord, not people, because you know that the Lord will reward each one for whatever good they do.

Ephesians 6:7–8

Christ's Blinding Light

"The only road to Christlikeness is to behold His goodness and beauty. We grow like what we look at, and if we spend our lives looking at our hateful selves, we will become more and more hateful. Looking at self, we are more and more changed into the image of self. While on the contrary, if we spend our time letting our minds dwell on God's goodness and love and trying to drink in His Spirit, the inevitable result will be that we will be changed into the image of the Lord."

$\mathcal{W}$e become what we focus on. Psychologically, this explains why a tyrannical parent may end up rearing tyrannical children. The children are so focused on the parent they are afraid of that despite their insistence later in life that they hated their father, they also become controlling and demanding. Thankfully, this principle also applies to loving parents; they are likely to produce loving children, because they've demonstrated this to their offspring.

We're also apt to become like the people we spend the most time with. Those who work with creative people may see their long-dormant creativity blossom. By the same token, it takes an exceptional person not to sink to new lows when working around negative people in a boring, dead-end job.

We can't always choose the people we work with, nor

can we be guaranteed a job in an exciting, inspirational environment. But we can decide what we choose to focus on. We can think night and day about the coworker who undermines us, or we can think about the God who loves us and wants both of us to experience His peace. We can focus our attention on the relative who harbors resentment for a decades-old offense, or we can turn our attention toward God, who placed us in the same family. God doesn't want us to dwell on the problem. He wants us to dwell with Him and let Him deal with our difficulties.

If we want to be like Christ, we need to spend time with Him. When we do, we find that negative people and situations fall away from our view. They haven't gone away; they've just grown dim in the way lesser objects become indistinct in the blinding sunlight. If we allow it, Christ's light can blind us to things we should never focus on anyway.

Fixing our eyes on Jesus, the pioneer and perfecter of faith.
For the joy set before him he endured the cross, scorning its shame,
and sat down at the right hand of the throne of God.

HEBREWS 12:2

"We should never indulge in any self-reflective acts, either of shame at our failures or of congratulation at our successes, but we should continually consign self and all self's doings to oblivion and keep our eyes on the Lord. It is very hard in self-examination not to try to find excuses for our faults; and our self-reflective acts are often in danger of being turned into self-glorying ones. They always do harm and never good. One of the most effective ways to conquer the habit is to make a rule that, whenever we are tempted to examine ourselves, we will immediately begin to examine the Lord instead and let thoughts of His love and His all-sufficiency sweep out all thoughts of our own unworthiness or helplessness."

During a heated confrontation with her adult daughter, a mother went too far, saying things she knew she should never say to her own child. Her words had been ugly and hurtful, completely out of character. After their conversation ended and her daughter left, the mother broke down in tears and began analyzing what had just happened. *I've always been a good person*, she thought. *Why would I lash out at my daughter like that?*

She went on to evaluate the hurtful things her daughter had said to her and wonder why she should stay out of her daughter's business. *I am her mother after all.* But then she realized that she knew better than to speak so spitefully and wished she could take back the errant words. But soon she was again thinking that her daughter had not shown her the honor she was due.

Whew! What did that mother gain from her introspection? Nothing of value, that's for certain. She became the judge and accuser of her daughter, she tried to justify what she did and said, she resorted to self-deprecation, and she glorified her position in her daughter's life. Not exactly a ringing endorsement of self-analysis, is it?

So if we shouldn't analyze our thoughts, words, and actions, who should? The answer is easy—the Holy Spirit. That's one of the reasons God sent His Spirit into our lives, to examine our hearts and show us the ugliness so we can allow Him to replace it with God's beauty. There's no point in us trying to ferret out the darkness in our hearts—but God's light, and that alone, can overcome the darkness.

What we have received is not the spirit of the world,
but the Spirit who is from God, so that we may
understand what God has freely given us.

1 CORINTHIANS 2:12

Discipline That Helps Us

"It might seem to those who don't understand the deepest ways of love that no trials or hardship could ever come into the lives of [God's] children. But if we look deeply into the matter, we will see that often love itself must bring the hardships. 'Whom the Lord loves he chastens, and scourges every son whom he receives. If you endure chastening, God deals with you as with sons; for what son is there whom a father does not chasten? But if are without chastening, of which all have become partakers, then you are illegitimate and not sons' (Hebrews 12:6–8)."

By the time his son turned eighteen months old, a first-time father was exasperated. He and his wife worked opposite shifts, and they had agreed on the need to discipline their child but never discussed how to do it. Now they seldom saw each other, and when they did, he did not want to admit he was overwhelmed. His nonconfrontational nature, gentle spirit, and deep love for his son translated into permissiveness; he could barely bring himself to say no, let alone put him in time-out.

Soon enough, his wife figured out why their child was defying her every chance he got. If it had happened only occasionally, she would have figured it was normal behavior for a child that age. But she couldn't get him to cooperate on anything. Knowing her husband's nature, she rightly concluded that he was being too lenient.

As she suspected, her husband confided that he equated discipline with harshness. "He's so little," her husband said. "I love him so much, and I want him to know that and not think I'm mean."

His wife paused. "Part of what it means to love him is to keep him from hurting himself—your no has to carry some weight when he's older and starts to run into the street," she said. "Another part is training him to be kind and cooperative when he's a child so he'll become the person God wants him to be." Once her husband realized how compatible love and discipline are, they were able to agree on specific methods of disciplining their son.

God's discipline—His distinct way of getting our attention when we're headed in the wrong direction—is always intended to help us and not hurt us. It's no fun, but it leads us to a place of joyful obedience—which is where God wanted us to be all along.

Blessed is the one you discipline, LORD, the one you teach from your law; you grant them relief from days of trouble.

PSALM 94:12–13

Some Things Must Go

"Because of His unfathomable love, the God of love,
when He sees His children resting their souls on things that can be shaken,
must remove those things from their lives in order that they may
be driven to rest only on the things that cannot be shaken.
And this process of removing is sometimes very hard."

Everyone experiences loss, but the way we react to loss depends on what was taken from us—and how much we relied on it for our happiness and security. Look at the way babies react when a beloved blankie needs to be washed. They wail at the top of their lungs! That blankie represents comfort to them, and they don't want to be deprived of it.

We may not wail loudly—at least hopefully not—but we adults can have a pretty strong reaction nonetheless when we lose something we treasure. With some losses, such as the death of a loved one, deep sorrow and mourning are to be expected. But what about when we lose something we never should have had in the first place, something that is hurting our lives? Shouldn't we be glad when those things are taken away?

Logic dictates that we should be, but that's not always the case. We know we should avoid toxic relationships, for example, but it's easy to become ensnared by them. A controlling and abusive spouse can shower you with words of love and promises to change, creating a harmful bond that is hard to break. An overbearing woman practically qualifies as a stalker but lays one guilt trip after another on a longsuffering friend who has sacrificed her own peace of mind because she desperately needs a friend. In each case, the "victim" has entered into an unhealthy, mutually dependent relationship that could prove traumatic when the perpetrator inevitably moves on to fresh prey.

Becoming excessively dependent on people, on jobs, on possessions, on anything we can lose is always unwise. Even while we may rely on them for support or financial security, we need to remember that they are transient. There is only one permanent, unshakable, immovable factor in our lives, and that's God and our relationship with Him. When things begin to interfere with our dependence on Him, we need to get rid of those things. If we don't, we can be fairly certain God will do it for us.

Depend on the LORD and his strength; always go to him for help.

1 CHRONICLES 16:11 NCV

Withstanding Life's Storms

"The house of the foolish man, which is built on the sand, may present a fine appearance in clear and sunshiny weather; but when storms arise, the winds blow, and floods come, that house will fall, and great will be the fall of it. The wise man's house, on the contrary, which is built on the rock, is able to withstand all the stress of the storm, and remains unshaken through winds and floods, for it is 'founded on the rock.' It is very possible in the Christian life to build one's spiritual house on such insecure foundations that when storms beat upon it, the ruin of that house is great. Many a religious experience that has seemed fair enough when all was going well in life has tottered and fallen when trials have come, because its foundations have been insecure. It is therefore of vital importance to each one of us to see to it that our religious life is built upon 'things that cannot be shaken.' "

When Superstorm Sandy tore through the East Coast in 2012, thousands of homes were destroyed or damaged. To the astonishment of many, the storm damage was erratic; a single home might be left standing in a neighborhood of houses that had been swept away by the power of water.

Much of the damage was inevitable, but some home-owners discovered to their horror that they had been victimized twice over—once by the forces of nature and before that by incompetent builders or unscrupulous housing inspectors. Their homes had not been built according to existing housing codes. Even a lesser storm would have done severe damage to those structures.

Most of us aren't builders or inspectors, so when we buy a house or other building, we have to trust that the people in charge are doing their jobs. When it comes to our spiritual life, though, we're in charge, and we're responsible for laying a solid foundation for our faith and building a solid spiritual life on it. And yes, we're also responsible for regular inspections; we accomplish that by inviting the Holy Spirit to shine His light on the areas of our lives that need close attention.

By spending time with God and getting to know Him intimately, we can be sure that the foundation for our faith will withstand life's storms because we are confident that He will see us through whatever turmoil we may face.

LORD, you alone are my portion and my cup;
you make my lot secure.

PSALM 16:5

"Conventionally we believe that Christ is the only Rock upon which to build, but practically, we believe that in order to have a rock upon which it will be really safe to build, many other things must be added to Christ. We think, for instance, that the right feelings must be added, or the right doctrines or dogmas, or whatever else may seem to each one of us to constitute the necessary degree of security. And if we were perfectly honest with ourselves, I suspect we should often find that our dependence was almost wholly upon these additions of our own, and that Christ Himself was of secondary importance. What we ought to mean when we talk about building on the Rock Christ Jesus is that the Lord is enough for our salvation, just the Lord without any additions of our own, the Lord Himself, as He is in His own intrinsic character, our Creator and Redeemer, and our all-sufficient portion."

When a Midwest pastor lost his job following a church split, he and his wife believed that his firing was a blessing in disguise. Finally, they would be able to start a church and share the role of minister. Within a few years, they had a thriving congregation. But some of the man's church-related decisions caused trouble for the church.

The problems began when the husband decided to teach a basic course on what it means to be a Christian and insisted that everyone in the church take the course—no exceptions. A few people objected, but none as adamantly as his wife. Soon, his insistence spread to other church activities. He "joked" that anyone who didn't sign up for the around-the-clock prayer chain could not be considered a Christian; the same was true for any adult who wasn't part of a service team and a small group. His wife tried to reason with him, but he was adamant.

He had added his own requirements to the simple matter of their faith in Christ. Church became a burden to congregants who worked long hours and had a strong, committed relationship with God. Implying that they were not "Christian enough" because they didn't follow man-made rules drove many away from his church.

Serving the church, learning about the faith, and participating in small groups are good, but none of those things will make us any more "Christian" than we already are. Our faith is built on Christ and Christ alone.

All the prophets testify about him that everyone who believes in him receives forgiveness of sins through his name.

ACTS 10:43

Getting Our Comeuppance

"There may be times in our religious lives when our experience seems to us as settled and immovable as the roots of the everlasting mountains. But then an upheaval comes and all our foundations are shaken and thrown down, and we are ready to despair and question whether we can be Christians at all."

The English language is full of colorful words and phrases, and many of them sound antiquated to our contemporary ears. One such word is *comeuppance*, which is seldom used but is something we all seem to get at one time or another. Getting our comeuppance isn't exactly a pleasant experience. When it happens, we know we've been beaten and gotten just what we deserve—usually some form of punishment or retribution in the wake of our arrogant behavior.

Arrogance, especially with regard to spiritual matters, should have no place in the life of one who claims to follow God. God considers humility to be of great value in His people; those who humble themselves before Him honor Him with their obedience. Arrogance is the opposite of humility; it reveals a haughtiness of spirit—in plain English, the spirit of a know-it-all.

Sadly we're all susceptible to it. We may think we're

immune, but we're not. Any time we declare *this* doctrine or *that* principle to be absolutely right, we're treading on dangerous ground, because we're setting ourselves up to be the final authority—and that's the height of arrogance. All we have to do is remember the church authorities who wanted Galileo put to death for the sacrilege of claiming that Earth is round. That should be enough to urge us to soften, if not kill, our insistence that we are right. If we don't, we're setting ourselves up for that inevitable time when we get our comeuppance—and when it comes, it's often in a very public manner.

God is the only final authority. We need to remember that whenever we start to argue about theology, social issues, or politics. Digging our heels in and insisting we are right won't help us win any arguments, nor will it bring any honor to God. We honor Him when we humbly admit that we don't know it all—but we know the one who does.

Who is wise and understanding among you?
Let them show it by their good life, by deeds done
in the humility that comes from wisdom.

JAMES 3:13

Pure, Living Water

"We seek to quench our thirst with our own experiences or our own activities, and then wonder why we still thirst. And it is to save us from perishing for lack of water that the Lord finds it necessary to destroy our broken cisterns, since only then can we be forced to drink from the fountain of living waters."

$\mathcal{F}$resh water is vital to our lives. We can't last more than a few days without it, and during that time we're likely to go mad with the mental effects of thirst and dehydration. Sailors on oceangoing vessels once feared running out of fresh water as much as they did any frightening creature of the sea; being surrounded by undrinkable saltwater only added to the torment they suffered if their freshwater supply was gone.

Jesus understood the necessity of fresh water when He compared Himself to "living water"—the spiritual refreshment that keeps our spirits alive. And yet, so many of us drink from contaminated wells and wonder why we don't feel refreshed; instead, we feel sick. So we go to a different contaminated well, drink from it, get sick, and still wonder why. We do the same things over and over again, expecting different results—a well-known definition of insanity.

But just what are the contaminated wells in our lives? They could be many things: unhealthy relationships, mind-numbing entertainment, costly and ultimately destructive habits, time-wasting activities that do nothing to enhance our lives, an unsettling fixation on money, even an obsession with education. Most "wells" are not bad in and of themselves; they become contaminated when we use them as a substitute for the real thing. Think of it this way: contaminated wells are like a murky, mosquito-infested swamp; living water is like a crystal-clear, cool mountain stream. Which should we drink from?

God no more wants us to drink from contaminated wells than He wants us to drink swamp water. He provided living water for us in the form of Jesus, and the bonus is that this well will never run dry. We can drink all night and day, and we will never experience spiritual thirst. Where do we find this living water? At Jesus' feet. When we spend time in His presence, in prayer, in His Word, we come away spiritually refreshed. Spiritual dehydration becomes a thing of the past.

"Whoever drinks the water I give them will never thirst.
Indeed, the water I give them will become in them
a spring of water welling up to eternal life."

JOHN 4:14

" 'We will not fear, even though the earth be removed, and though the mountains be carried into the midst of the sea; though the waters roar and be troubled, though the mountains shake with its swelling. . . . God is in the midst of her, she shall not be moved. God shall help her, just at the break of dawn' (Psalm 46:2–3, 5). Can it be possible that we, who are so easily moved by the things of earth, can arrive at a place where nothing can upset our temper or disturb our calm?"

When a Florida family's home and garage were swallowed by a sinkhole, destroying all their possessions, onlookers were surprised to see the mother and father going around town just a few days later, consoling friends who expected to be consoling them. Even the two children returned to high school and assured their friends that everything was fine.

Some people began to think the family was in shock and would need therapy to recover from the disaster. But those who knew the family well were not surprised by their serenity. Their friends knew exactly why their home's destruction meant so little to them: this was the second time they had been left with nothing.

The first time, however, had been different in a significant way. "Losing" everything had been intentional. Prompted by reports of a dangerous shortage of clean water in central Africa, they spent considerable time exploring the situation and seeking God's guidance about helping out in a tangible way. Once they got the green light, they sold or donated everything they owned, apart from the few things they could take with them. Both parents were engineers and had signed on with a nonprofit that was working on a variety of methods of getting fresh water to remote villages. For three years they lived as the people in the area lived. By the time they returned to the States, they were detached from the desire to acquire material possessions and had never become attached to the things the earth eventually swallowed.

When we become attached to people, places, or things, we risk losing our peace when those things are taken away. Learning to detach can take a lifetime, even for those who are committed to the concept. We must first learn to attach ourselves to God alone. When everything else in our lives is shaken, our attachment to God will find us on solid ground.

Jesus answered, "If you want to be perfect, go, sell your possessions and give to the poor, and you will have treasure in heaven. Then come, follow me."

MATTHEW 19:21

" "Therefore, since we are receiving a kingdom which cannot be shaken, let us have grace, by which we may serve God acceptably with reverence and godly fear. For our God is a consuming fire' (Hebrews 12:28–29). Many people are afraid of the consuming fire of God, but that is only because they don't understand what it is. It is the fire of God's love that must consume everything that can harm His people; and if our hearts are set on being what the love of God would have us be, His fire is something we won't be afraid of but will warmly welcome."

The image of being refined by fire isn't a pleasant one. For any metal to be purified, extremely high temperatures are required. Knowing how full of impurities we are, we shouldn't ever be surprised when God turns up the heat on us in order to refine us.

As painful as the refining process is, it becomes a bit easier when we acknowledge that the fire is necessary. Many people don't think it is; they believe human beings are essentially good. They come up with any number of excuses for the evil in the world, and for each excuse, they come up with countless ways evil can be reversed or eradicated or cured. But the reality is that the rest of us have looked deep inside ourselves and recognized the evil that is resident there. We realize that left to our own devices, we would quickly dispel the myth of humanity's inherent goodness.

God's refining fire is the only hope we have if we genuinely want to get rid of the impurities in our lives. By cooperating with the refining process, it's likely to go more quickly because we aren't holding back and trying to hide our sin from God. It's as if we're saying, "Here I am, God—do with me what You will." But if we try to fight the fire, we prolong the agony because we'll just have to stay in the furnace longer.

It's no fun being purified. But one of the end results is joy, the joy that comes from finally being rid of the sins that have made our lives miserable. If all it takes to achieve that is God's refining fire, then it's well worth the pain.

The fire shall try every man's work of what sort it is.
If any man's work abide which he hath built thereupon,
he shall receive a reward.

1 CORINTHIANS 3:13–14 KJV

"To be 'pleasant' and 'delightful' to the Lord may seem to us impossible, when we look at our shortcomings and our unworthiness. But when we think of this lovely, consuming fire of God's love, we can be of good heart and take courage, for He will not fail or be discouraged until all our dross is burned up and we come forth in His likeness and are conformed to His image."

Shortly after her mother's death, an art student returned to university to finish up her second semester. In one of her classes, students were challenged to draw a self-portrait, without using a mirror or photograph of themselves as a guide. The portrait could be as abstract, realistic, or whimsical as the student felt it should be.

This particular student set out to draw a true-to-life depiction of herself. She made several attempts at the eyes until they were just right. The nose was easy; she hated her nose and knew just how crooked it was. The mouth—that was hard. Despite the number of times she had applied lipstick over the years, she couldn't quite remember how full her lips were. She did her best, turned in the drawing, and got a decent grade.

After the drawing was returned to her, she taped it to her dorm room wall so she could assess her skills.

"Oh, what a lovely drawing of your mother!" Her roommate, who had spent several weekends at her house during the year, was clearly taken by the likeness. The artist objected; that was a self-portrait, not a drawing of her mother. "No, it's your mother," the roommate insisted. "The hairstyle is yours, but the face is your mother's."

She was right. The art student missed her mother so much that in her mind's eye, all she could see was the face of the woman she had loved since before she understood the meaning of love. In her imagination, her own face had morphed into her mother's; she bore her mother's likeness.

We were created in God's image, but our human nature takes over and obscures that image until it is barely recognizable. We all need to be transformed into His image. As with the art student, the longer we focus on His image and the deeper our love for Him, the more we become like Him. To be conformed to His image requires a longing for Him that overtakes all other desires.

God created humankind in his image, in the image of God he created them; male and female he created them.

GENESIS 1:27 NRSV

Barriers to Our Faith

*"The Bible declares that faith is the law of the spiritual life,
and that according to our faith it always will be unto us. Then, since
faith and discouragement cannot exist together, it is perfectly clear that
discouragement must be a barrier to faith. And where discouragement rules,
the converse to the law of faith must rule also, and it will be to us, not
according to our faith, but according to our discouragement."*

With so many potential barriers to our faith, we should know better than to build obstructions of our own. But whenever we allow discouragement to set in, that is exactly what happens. We put up an obstacle that prevents us from exercising our faith.

Maybe we became discouraged after praying for months that a friend's marriage would be restored. But now after a year of praying, things have only gotten worse. *It's no use,* we think. We lose faith. We stop praying—unknowingly, just at the point when our friend feels she cannot live with the uncertainty any longer. She needs to make a decision about whether to file for divorce. When our friend needs our prayers and support the most, our discouragement has caused us to give up.

We will never know how much our lack of faith has impacted other people, just as we will never fully understand the power of prayer this side of heaven. But we do know that it matters, and if we need scientific proof, it's there for the asking; although medical and scientific studies can't explain how it works, they report that it does. Most of us don't need outside proof, though. In our own lives, we have experienced the effectiveness of a prayer that is grounded in faith. When discouragement blocks our faith, it blocks our prayers as well—because unless we're asking God to free us from being discouraged, we're not likely to be doing much praying.

We can avoid becoming discouraged by not having faith in circumstances. What we see with our eyes—the circumstances surrounding us—doesn't matter. It's hard to wrap our heads around that sometimes, but what matters is the unseen realm where God is at work—and where there's no room for discouragement.

You, LORD, hear the desire of the afflicted;
you encourage them, and you listen to their cry.

PSALM 10:17

> _"Discouragement cannot have its source in God. The religion of_
> _the Lord Jesus Christ is a religion of faith, of good cheer, of courage,_
> _of hope that doesn't disappoint. 'Be discouraged,' says our lower nature,_
> _'for the world is a place of temptation and sin.' 'Be of good cheer,' says_
> _Christ, 'for I have overcome the world.' There cannot possibly be any_
> _room for discouragement in a world that Christ has overcome."_

It's been said that if we could recognize and understand our capacity for greatness, each person on earth could achieve unimaginable accomplishments. Whether that's true cannot be proven, but a variation on that idea is certainly true—many of us never reach our potential because we lack the confidence and assurance that we can succeed at being better than we are. We hold ourselves back.

Discouragement keeps us stuck. If we become disheartened because we missed out on a promotion that we felt we deserved, we're likely to remain stuck in our present job because we lack the motivation to seek a promotion the next time an opportunity arises. Artists of every kind are especially susceptible to the paralyzing effect of discouragement; the artist who hasn't sold a single watercolor in months, the actor who waits tables to pay the rent, the novelist whose sales have tanked often find themselves unable to pick up a paintbrush, go for an audition, or write a word, all because they have given up. They are so discouraged that they begin to question their talent.

Meanwhile, angels in heaven are cheering them on, but they're so downcast that they would never believe it. We know from the Bible that there's a cheering section in heaven urging us on. And God Himself is always encouraging us—comforting us when we're down but also extending a hand to help us get back on our feet again.

If we truly believe that Christ has overcome the world and that He has invited us to participate in His life, then we need to believe that through the power of Christ we can overcome as well. There's no longer any reason for us to be depressed by life's failures. Christ has given us Himself, and in Him lies everything we need to overcome any discouragement we may face.

Whatsoever is born of God overcometh the world:
and this is the victory that overcometh the world, even our faith.

1 JOHN 5:4 KJV

Victory in Every Battle

"To all words of discouragement in the Bible this is the invariable answer, 'I will be with you,' and it is an answer that precludes all possibility of argument or of any further discouragement. I your Creator and Redeemer, your strength and wisdom, your omnipresent and omniscient God, I will be with you and will protect you through everything. No enemy shall hurt you, no strife of tongues shall disturb you; My presence shall be your safety and your sure defense."

Discouragement doesn't just come upon us when we're striving for something we want to accomplish or hoping for something good to happen. It also settles in on us when we're fighting a battle that appears hopeless.

Parents of drug addicts know that sense of hopelessness. The power of drug addiction over an individual can turn a promising valedictorian into a homeless junkie or a young mother into a street hustler in a matter of months. It's frightening to think of how quickly people's lives can hit rock bottom when they begin taking meth in particular; their loved ones embark on a fierce but often losing battle, and it's nearly impossible to keep discouragement at bay.

Many of us fight far less dangerous battles every day, but still, they affect our faith and our mental and emotional well-being. Chronic pain, disability, and the ordinary effects of aging can wreak havoc on our efforts to fight for the quality of life we once knew.

But whether our battles are life-threatening or life-altering, we must never lose sight of the fact that God is always present and fights for us. When we're already weakened by our own pain or the pain of seeing a loved one suffer, what makes us think we have the strength to fight? We don't, and we won't win anyway if we rely on what little strength we have.

No doubt about it, we can be a forgetful people at times. We forget that God has promised to protect us and defend us against anything that tries to attack us. We forget that there is nothing in this world or any other world that is more powerful than God. We forget that He is ever present, on the battlefield and off. He is the antidote for discouragement in every battle we face.

I am the LORD your God who takes hold of your right hand and says to you, Do not fear; I will help you.

ISAIAH 41:13

Entering God's Rest

*"Do we not look at our weakness instead of the Lord's strength,
and have we not sometimes become so discouraged that we cannot even
listen to the Lord's own declarations that He will fight for us and will give
us the victory? Our souls long to enter into the rest the Lord has promised,
but giants and cities great and fortified up to heaven seem
to stand in our way, and we are afraid to believe."*

The Lord's rest can seem like a foreign concept. We can barely manage to squeeze in the physical rest we need during a typical twenty-four-hour cycle. Who has time to even imagine what the Lord's rest actually looks like, let alone enter into it?

But we can't deny that it is possible, or God would not have promised it to us. Maybe we consider it an impossibility because we really don't understand it. We think of "rest" as an extended break from activity, like taking a long nap on a rainy day or lazing in a hammock on a summer afternoon. But the beauty of the Lord's rest is that we can enter into it at any time, even when we're stuck in rush-hour traffic, scrambling to meet a deadline, or running to catch a flight.

In a sense, the Lord's rest is active. We intentionally enter into it by activating our faith and taking a deep spiritual breath. We say to God, "Okay, Lord, this is it. This traffic is driving me up a wall, but I need to stay on the road! I need Your peace to fall on me now. Help me enter into Your rest." It's this deliberate turning to God and trusting Him to calm our spirits that can make all the difference in our day and in our lives.

There may be giants—seemingly insurmountable problems—all around us trying to block God's rest from reaching us and permeating our lives, but nothing, absolutely nothing, can prevent God from showering His rest on us. Whether we allow that shower to fall on us is another matter altogether. Will we look at the giants and our inability to defeat them, or will we look to God, who will calm our spirits as He goes about slaying the giants for us?

[Jesus said to his disciples,] "Come to me, all you that are weary and are carrying heavy burdens, and I will give you rest. . . I am gentle and humble in heart, and you will find rest for your souls."

MATTHEW 11:28–29 NRSV

"If I see myself to be a sinner, how can I help being discouraged? To this I answer that the Holy Spirit does not convict us of sin in order to discourage us but to encourage us. His work is to show us our sin, not that we may lie down in despair under its power but that we may get rid of it. Surely then when God says to us, 'Though your sins are like scarlet, they shall be as white as snow' (Isaiah 1:18), it is pure unbelief on our part to allow ourselves to be discouraged at even the worst of our failures."

When the city manager of a small municipality was caught embezzling city funds, residents demanded he be brought to justice. Some of his political opponents called for blood, but cooler heads prevailed, and he was fired, tried, convicted, and punished. After paying his debt, he and his wife decided to stay in the same town despite his reputation as a thief. Everyone wondered why.

What "everyone" didn't know was that the embezzler had met God. In desperation he prayed to a God he wasn't sure existed and asked Him to reveal Himself. What happened next stunned him into submission to God, because suddenly he felt soapy water being poured all over him. The sensation was so real that even though his eyes were wide open and he was perfectly dry, he asked his wife to assure him that his eyes weren't deceiving him. He told her he could feel the lather cascading over him. She burst out laughing and said, "I just prayed that God would cleanse you of your sin and shame!"

His wife encouraged him, at that moment and for the rest of their lives. They stayed on in town because they felt if they left they would be running from his misconduct. They loved the town and wanted to walk blamelessly in it once again.

It's hard to stand tall once we've been beaten down by our own sin. God never wants us to wallow in the misdeeds of the past; He wants us to get up and walk in His ways toward a brighter future. The Holy Spirit is always right there with us to make sure we know what God's ways are—and where they lead.

Let the wicked forsake their ways and the unrighteous their thoughts.
Let them turn to the LORD, and he will have mercy on them,
and to our God, for he will freely pardon.

ISAIAH 55:7

Mending the Brokenness

*"We know from experience that courage is contagious and that one
really brave soul in moments of danger can save a crowd from a panic.
But we too often fail to remember that the converse of this is true,
and that one fainthearted man or woman can infect a whole crowd
with fear. We consequently think nothing of expressing with the utmost
freedom the discouragements that are paralyzing our own courage.
'Be of good cheer' is the command of the Lord for His disciples,
under all circumstances, and He founded this command on
the tremendous fact that He had overcome the world."*

The world looked on in shock when several explosions rocked
the festivities at the finish line of the Boston Marathon in
April of 2013. Despite widespread confusion and panic, the
chaos that could have led to more deaths and injuries was
largely avoided as courageous athletes, spectators, and trained
emergency personnel acted quickly and calmly to clear the
area and get the injured to the medical tent.

Their fearless service was underscored by the fact that
they did not know if more devices were about to be detonated.
They could have died in their attempts to save others, but they
continued their efforts nonetheless.

The sight of several dozen people running toward the

point of detonation rather than away from it inspired observers around the world. Footage of their heroic acts played repeatedly on televisions and computers worldwide. And frequently the question was asked, "What makes some people rush to help while risking their own lives?" The answers they got from the helpers they interviewed almost consistently pointed to an impulse—they responded instinctively to the need without thinking about their own safety. They looked outward rather than inward.

Looking inward often results in fear. We look inside ourselves and see ineptitude and vulnerability. We're afraid to risk our comfort and our safety. Let's face it: ultimately, we're afraid to die. But if we believe that Jesus has overcome the world, we should have no reason to fear anything. That may seem like a radical statement, but it's true. No reason to fear anything—not a terrorist attack or a tornado or a rattlesnake bite. Nothing.

As long as we have the wisdom to take necessary precautions, we can have the courage to run toward the broken people of the world. There we will see Jesus at work, mending the brokenness that evil has caused.

I have told you these things, so that in me you may have peace.
In this world you will have trouble.
But take heart! I have overcome the world.

JOHN 16:33

Speaking Truth about God

"How different it would be if discouragement were looked upon in its true light as a 'speaking against God,' and only encouraging words were permitted among Christians and encouraging reports heard! Who can tell how many spiritual defeats and disasters your discouragements may have brought about in your own life and in the lives of those around you?"

$\mathcal{I}$f we considered discouragement as "speaking against God," how would that affect our speech? Some would say that our refusal to acknowledge our discouragement would be dishonest; we shouldn't say everything is fine if it isn't. But aren't there ways to be encouraging to others even if we are disheartened in our relationship with God?

Of course there are, but some of us need more training than others in how to be an encouragement when we're struggling to reassure ourselves. It's vital to be an encourager because we'll most likely be on the receiving end of our own positive words; in other words, as we uplift others, we ourselves will be encouraged. So many spiritual principles work that way, but we shouldn't be surprised. It was Jesus Himself who pointed out that we reap what we sow. If we sow encouragement, that's what we'll reap.

There's no question that there's a fine line between

dishonesty and speaking positive words when we're not feeling very optimistic. But as Christians, we walk fine lines all the time. We don't have to say things are going great when they're not; people can see right through our faux perkiness. That's like telling people we feel fantastic when we're running a 102-degree fever and coughing so much that our throat and lungs are burning—no one would believe us. But we can say God has been faithful in whatever difficulties we're going through. That's an encouragement, that's positive, and that's the truth.

Insincerity is transparent. We don't need to resort to that. But if we speak the truth about God and His activity in our lives, even when we are bordering on despair and looking to God to pull us out of it, we bring light to others, and that light is reflected back on us.

Whoever sows to please the Spirit,
from the Spirit will reap eternal life.

GALATIANS 6:8

No Loss, Only Gain

"If I am asked how we are to get rid of discouragements, I can only say that we must give them up. It is never worthwhile to argue against discouragement. There is only one argument that can meet it, and that is the argument of God. When David was in the midst of what were perhaps the most discouraging moments of his life, when he had found his city burned and his wives stolen, and he and the men with him had wept until they could weep no more; and when his men, exasperated at their misfortunes, spoke of stoning him, then we are told, 'David encouraged himself in the LORD his God' (1 Samuel 30:6). The result was a magnificent victory, in which all that they had lost was more than restored to them. This always will be the result of a courageous faith, because faith lays hold of the omnipotence of God."

One little girl had such a sensitive nature that her parents worried how she would handle a significant loss, given that minor losses—a treasured toy, a friend who moved to a different neighborhood—had affected her so deeply. So when her beloved grandmother was diagnosed with end-stage cancer and placed in hospice care, her parents grew concerned.

Within a few months, her grandmother died. The little girl's eyes began to water when she was told, and she asked to be left alone. Her parents, who were dealing with their own grief, complied, though they kept her door open so they could hear if she became too distraught. What they heard stunned them.

"Jesus, I understand. I won't see her again for a long time. I guess that's it," she said. She wiped her tears, stood quietly for a moment, and joined her parents.

"It's okay," she said. "Can I go to preschool now?"

Children are amazingly resilient. The same little girl who cried over a doll her puppy mangled accepted her grandmother's death with unusual composure; she talked to Jesus and left it there. As adults, we are not quite that resilient when it comes to the death of a loved one; our lives are intertwined with theirs in a complex way, and that makes the grief tough to recover from. But if only we could "encourage ourselves in the Lord our God," get up off the floor, and resume our lives knowing that the Lord is there to comfort us as we go.

My soul is downcast within me. Yet this I call to mind and therefore I have hope: Because of the LORD's great love we are not consumed, for his compassions never fail. They are new every morning; great is your faithfulness.

LAMENTATIONS 3:20–23

Calming the Disquiet

"Over and over the psalmist asks himself this question:
'Why are you cast down, O my soul? And why are you disquieted
within me?' And each time he answers himself with the argument of God:
'Hope in God, for I shall yet praise Him for the help of His countenance'
(Psalm 42:5). He does not analyze his discouragement or try to argue it
away, but he turns at once to the Lord and by faith begins to praise Him."

*D*isquiet is a word that we don't hear often in ordinary
conversation. But what a descriptive word it is! The disquiet in
our souls is a result of all the noise around us and in us—the
cacophony of sounds that robs us of our peace and disturbs
our sense of well-being. The most harmful of those sounds are
the words of judgment and criticism that have been spoken
against us.

"You'll never amount to anything!" When spoken by a
parent, this can have devastating results.

"What makes you think she would ever go out with you?"
A friend laughs as he says this, but he's dead serious.

"You'll never make it to our top design team." A graphic
artist replays those words in her head every day, no matter how
hard she tries not to.

Those kinds of sounds are the most troubling cause of

disquiet within us—the words of others that echo through our minds. But there is a way to get rid of them. Since it's impossible to think two thoughts at the same time, we simply have to replace the negative thoughts with positive ones. The most effective and spiritually positive thoughts are words of praise to God.

When we turn our hearts toward God and start to praise Him, we reduce the unrest within us. Eventually, as we acquire the habit of praising Him, the disquiet is replaced by the peace of God. We don't have to try to discipline ourselves to be less discouraged or undergo psychoanalysis to figure out why those words spoken by that particular person disturb us so much. Once we recognize that the people who uttered those words are just as broken as we are, we can forget about trying to solve the problem ourselves and get on with what we were always meant to do—praise God at all times.

Let everything that has breath praise the LORD.
Praise the LORD!

PSALM 150:6 NKJV

Grateful Path to Joy

"Thanksgiving or complaining—these words express two contrasting attitudes of the souls of God's children in regard to His dealings with them, and they are more powerful than we are inclined to believe. The soul that gives thanks can find comfort in everything; the soul that complains can find comfort in nothing."

*A*n elderly man who lived alone on a long-dormant farm had a smile and a cheerful word for everyone. When he was home, he would take a kitchen chair and an umbrella down by the highway and sit there all day, smiling and waving at everyone who drove by. The umbrella shielded him from sun and rain and sometimes even snow, unless it was so cold he had to stay inside. When he drove his rusty old pickup into town, he'd stop in just about every store and greet customers and owners, strangers and familiar faces and long-time friends.

A local reporter figured the farmer had a slew of stories to tell, and he was right. As they sat by the highway—the farmer insisted he be interviewed there so he wouldn't miss a day of waving at drivers—the elderly man told the reporter about happy times as well as difficult ones, like the crop-killing droughts and locust infestations, the death of his wife, and the morning he had to admit his farming days were over. The reporter noticed that he expressed gratitude for everything, even the bad times.

"I guess you could say you had a rosy way of looking at things, right?" the reporter said.

The man looked at him as if he was surprised anyone could think such an outlandish thing. "Why, no," he said. "I just kept thanking God for the good things and the bad, and the next thing I knew, I was plumb happy all the time!"

The link between gratitude and joy is indisputable. Joyful people are thankful people, not because everything is going great but because their gratitude creates a spirit of joyfulness. They've learned that they don't have to be happy about something to thank God for it; they've learned instead to thank God that He's in charge and they're not, because He knows what He's doing and they don't. Complaining feeds a grumpy nature, but gratitude—that fosters a joyful spirit, one that recognizes God's hand in our lives.

> *In everything give thanks; for this is the will*
> *of God in Christ Jesus for you.*

1 THESSALONIANS 5:18 NKJV

Expressing Thanks to God

"God's command is 'in everything give thanks,' and the command is emphasized by the declaration 'for this is the will of God in Christ Jesus for you' (1 Thessalonians 5:18). It is an actual positive command, and if we want to obey God, we simply have to give thanks in everything."

Some of us treat the Bible verse admonishing us to thank God in every situation as if we were choosing upgrades for a new car: "Well, let's see—I'll take faith in Jesus Christ along with the generosity option, but let's forget about the thankfulness package. I don't think I need that." We do need it, and it's a standard feature of the Christian life. Without it, we fail to express to God our gratefulness for everything that we have and everything that happens in our lives, both the seen and the unseen.

A spirit of gratitude keeps us humble. When we show others that we are grateful for their presence in our lives, we acknowledge that our lives are better because of them. When we thank people from our hearts for the tangible gifts they have given us, we recognize their thoughtfulness and generosity. When we express gratitude to people for their spiritual influence on our lives, we're telling them that we would not be the God-loving, God-following people we are today without them.

Expressing our gratitude to God is even more vital in keeping us humble. If He is truly our Lord, we don't have a leg to stand on when we try to prop ourselves up on a pedestal, pointing to our achievements in a feeble attempt at self-glorification. When we live as if He is our Lord, knowing that what others see as our achievements are all thanks to God working in us, then we don't even want a pedestal; to place ourselves on it, or allow others to do so, would be an act of fraud.

Gratitude is in our Christian DNA. To try to separate it out and treat it as an option simply won't succeed—because one day, when we've reached the end of ourselves and we know we deserve the worst punishment we can ever imagine, we'll experience the love and forgiveness of God once again, and our hearts will be filled with a sense of gratitude like we've never known before.

Enter into His gates with thanksgiving, and into His courts with praise. Be thankful to Him, and bless His name.

PSALM 100:4 NKJV

137

Gratitude in Disastrous Times

"It is true we cannot always give thanks for [all] things themselves,
but we can always give thanks for God's love and care in the things.
He may not have ordered them, but He is in them somewhere,
and He is in them to compel them to work together for our good."

Sometimes it's the littlest words that can trip us up the most. The Internet is replete with funny words and phrases that people have misheard and repeated online. Frequently, though, it's not our hearing that's the problem. It's our understanding, and the results can be far from comical.

At a family dinner that was always a hotbed of political conversation, the topic turned to faith—and just about everyone took a deep breath, because they knew what was coming.

"You Christians! You say we should thank God for everything! Well, you tell me—why should I thank God for my son getting killed in Afghanistan?" one of the older men said.

Everyone remained silent. His grief was still so raw, all these years later. His daughter-in-law, the soldier's widow, was the first to speak.

"It says 'in,'" she said quietly, noticing the puzzled looks around the table. "The Bible verse—it says 'in everything give thanks,' not 'for.'"

Her father-in-law held his tongue when he saw her bottom lip start to quiver.

"I didn't thank God that my husband died," she said. "How anyone could think that is beyond me. I learned to thank God in everything that's happened since then—his body coming back, learning to live without him, trying to raise a child who misses his daddy so much. I thank God for the strength He's given me to just stay alive."

She understood the distinction between those two short words—*in* and *for*. Does God expect us to thank Him for a tornado that killed a dozen people, devastated a town, and upended the lives of countless people? No. But He does want us to express our gratitude to Him in the midst of the worst storms that affect our lives.

Like the widow, we always have plenty to thank God for. When we get in the habit of thanking Him for our blessings during the good times, then thanking Him in times of devastation and loss becomes second nature. And that's a result of tending to our spiritual condition throughout our lives.

O give thanks to the LORD, for he is good,
for his steadfast love endures forever.

PSALM 136:1 NRSV

"We can all remember, I think, similar instances in our own lives when God has made the wrath of man to praise Him and has caused even the hardest trials to work together for our greatest good. I recall once in my own life when a trial was brought on me by another person, at which I was filled with bitter rebellion and could not see in it from beginning to end anything to be thankful for. But that very trial worked out for me the richest blessings and the greatest triumphs of my whole life; and in the end I was filled with thanksgiving for the very things that had caused me such bitter rebellion before. If only I had had faith enough to give thanks at first, how much sorrow would have been spared me."

During times of economic downturn, most consumers drastically change their buying habits. They have less expendable income, either because of the high price of essentials like gas and food or because of layoffs or reduced hours at work. It's not a hard-and-fast rule, but frequently one of the few segments of the economy that does well during a recession is the religious publishing industry.

The same often holds true following tragedies and cataclysmic events. Many see this as a clear indication that during difficult times, people are willing to spend what little money they can on books that offer answers to their questions about God. They need hope, and they're counting on religious books to provide it.

God uses whatever it takes to get our attention. While He doesn't orchestrate these tragic events, He does use them to turn our hearts toward Him. We could avoid so much pain and heartache if only we stayed close to Him when things are going well, but that's when we're most likely to forget Him.

Then what do we do? We blame God. *Why isn't He here when we need Him? Why has He abandoned us in this horrible situation?* Well, He's right here. He never abandoned us. We simply failed to realize that we always need Him.

If we could only see with eyes of faith in every circumstance, how much better our lives would be! We would look at the storm clouds and see sunshine; in place of our lack we would see abundance. We can never forget God's assurance that everything works together for our good—everything.

We know that in all things God works for the good of those who love him, who have been called according to his purpose.

ROMANS 8:28

"I am afraid that the greatest height most Christians in their shortsightedness seem able to rise is to strive after resignation to things they cannot alter and to seek for patience to endure them. The result is that thanksgiving is almost an unknown exercise among the children of God."

For most of history, herbal remedies were the only medicines available, and for the most part they were harmless and effective, to varying degrees. When the production of synthetic and chemical drugs began, some people were understandably skeptical about ingesting medication created in a laboratory. What kind of witchcraft was this?

By the time chemical pain relievers became widely available, consumers had come to trust the safety of such medications, but there were a fair number of holdouts. One man in his seventies who had suffered from headaches his entire life was among those who put no stock in the products of pharmaceutical labs.

His doctor had ordered numerous tests and referred the man to specialists. He found no organic cause for the pain, and still the man suffered. Aware of his patient's refusal to take pain relievers, he devised an alternate plan.

"I've done everything I know to do for you. I have to

release you from my care. Maybe you can find a doctor who can do you some good."

"There's nothing you can do? Are you sure?"

"Yes, but there's something you can do."

"Anything. I'll do anything. I don't want to start all over with a different doctor."

"Then take the aspirin I've been prescribing for the last twenty years."

That night, the stubborn patient gave in—and finally found relief. Every day for decades, he had needlessly endured chronic pain by not trusting his doctor.

God offers us comfort and relief from the pain in our lives, but instead of trusting Him to provide it, we stubbornly refuse His help. We're strong; we can handle it. Besides, aren't Christians supposed to suffer? We resign ourselves to misery and put on a brave face—often, an unpleasant one—as we endure the anguish. All the while, God has been holding out to us the remedy for all our suffering—His presence. Who would choose discomfort when relief is at hand? God's offer never expires; we can grab hold of it now and see an end to our pain.

Let the wise also hear and gain in learning,
and the discerning acquire skill.

PROVERBS 1:5 NRSV

"Complaining is always alike, whether it is on the temporal or the spiritual plane. It always has in it the element of fault finding. Webster says to complain means 'to make a charge or an accusation.' It is not merely disliking the thing we have to bear, but it contains the element of finding fault with the agency that lies behind it. And if we will carefully examine the true nature of our complainings, I think we will generally find they are founded on a subtle faultfinding with God. We secretly feel as if He were to blame somehow, and almost unconsciously to ourselves, we make mental charges against Him."

Most people probably don't realize that complaining means faultfinding. We complain about traffic, finding fault with construction crews, highway engineers, and other drivers on the road. We complain about the officer who pulled us over for speeding, blaming her for the fact that we got a ticket for breaking the law. We complain about the weather, never realizing that we're finding fault with the one who created atmospheric conditions. We never have a shortage of things to complain about, but we don't make the connection between our complaints and the accusations we're making against others.

Turn the tables, though, and when our spouse complains

about something we're only partially responsible for, we readily assume it's an accusation against us. In our minds, an innocent comment about the steak being tough is never about the cut of meat; it's about the way we cooked it. If we would be as quick to give others the benefit of the doubt as we are to take offense, our lives would be so much more peaceful—just as they would be if we were as quick to express gratitude as we are to complain.

Constant carping robs us and everyone around us of the peace God wants us to have. It also dishonors God, who has given us an amazing life on an amazing planet among amazing people. Sure, there's a lot that isn't so amazing, but on any given day, more things go right than wrong. Instead of complaining because it's raining, let's thank God for the awesomeness of how well the universe and everything in it works together. God has given us so much! Let's always choose to be thankful.

Give thanks to the LORD, for he is good; his love endures forever.

1 CHRONICLES 16:34

God's Wounded Heart

"It is very evident from the whole teaching of Scripture that the Lord loves to be thanked and praised just as much as we like it. I am sure that it gives Him downright pleasure and that our failure to thank Him for His 'good and perfect gifts' wounds His loving heart, just as our hearts are wounded when our loved ones fail to appreciate the benefits we have so enjoyed bestowing on them."

Praise is something most people lap up, especially when they think it's well-deserved—whether it is or not. And why wouldn't we enjoy the praise of others? If we've worked hard and done our best at something, it's great to have others acknowledge our success. But it's dangerous to believe we're as great as they say we are; we get into trouble when pride starts to take over.

Young children offer a great example of the way we adults should respond to the praise of others. What does a toddler do when his mother praises him for putting away his toys? He looks as pleased as punch and says something like, "I'm Mommy's big helper!" He's happy that he did a big-boy task and made Mommy proud. And then he just goes back to being a toddler. If only we could react the same way. What an accomplishment that would be!

Since we enjoy praise so much, and we're made in the image of God, it's fair to say that He enjoys praise as well. We gain a deeper understanding of God when we begin to think of praising Him as something He receives and enjoys rather than something we do. In fact, if we're still carrying around the image of God as a stern judge, we may be so self-conscious in our attempts at praise, wondering if we're doing it right, that we never offer Him the raw praise that comes from a heart of gratitude.

It may be hard to think of God as having a wounded heart, but our praise of Him would likely be more frequent and more authentic if we did. It's so much better to think of His heart filled with joy when we come before Him just to tell Him how much we love Him and how thankful we are for all He's done.

I will praise God in a song and will honor him by giving thanks.

PSALM 69:30 NCV

Saving Our Spiritual Lives

"Even when we realize that things come directly from God, we find it very hard to give thanks for what hurts us. Do we not, however, all know what it is to thank a skillful physician for his treatment of our diseases, even though that treatment may have been very severe? And surely we should no less give thanks to our divine Physician when He is obliged to give us bitter medicine to cure our spiritual diseases or perform a painful operation to rid us of something that harms."

As a breast cancer patient was undergoing her second round of chemotherapy, she wondered if it was worth it. The nausea and fatigue that followed her treatments were almost more than she could bear. Already underweight before the cancer was diagnosed, she barely had the stamina to make it through each day. She could only hope that the chemo was working. For two years, she and her medical team fought hard to keep the disease at bay.

Years later she crossed the stage at a Susan G. Komen event and received recognition for being cancer-free for five years. Asked to say a few words to the crowd in attendance, she said, "A few words? Yes, it was worth it." Cancer survivors and their caregivers knew exactly what she meant; it was worth the aftereffects of chemo, radiation, and surgery to be standing on that stage, fully alive.

To be fully alive spiritually may require that we take a dose of foul-tasting medicine to cure the diseases that have infected our spirits. Anger, envy, lust—they're just a few of the disorders that poison our soul, and the antidote may be severe. Uncontrolled anger has caused many people to make fools of themselves, and the prescribed treatment for envy may be to have our possessions stripped away from us. Lust? The only cure may be the threat of losing the people who mean the most to us, our spouse and children.

A bitter pill to swallow is more than a familiar expression. It's an apt description of what God may have to give us in order to cure the spiritual diseases that keep us from walking in harmony with Him. Just as a breast cancer survivor will gladly give thanks for the treatment that saved her life, so we should gladly give thanks to God for saving our spiritual life—and so much more.

Everything God made is good,
and nothing should be refused if it is accepted with thanks.

1 TIMOTHY 4:4 NCV

Praising God Continually

"The psalmist says: 'I will praise the name of God with a song, and will magnify him with thanksgiving. This also shall please the Lord better than an ox or bull, which has horns and hoofs' (Psalm 69:30–31). Many people seem quite ready and willing to offer up some great sacrifice to the Lord but never seem to realize that a little genuine praise and thanksgiving offered to Him now and then would 'please Him better' than all their great sacrifices made in His cause."

You just don't appreciate me!" a visibly disenchanted wife complained to her husband. "I've given up everything for you! I gave up my career, my friends, everything!"

Her husband remained silent.

"Aren't you going to say anything? See what I mean? You can't even acknowledge the sacrifices I've made for you!"

After a few moments of silence, her husband said quietly, "But I never asked you to do any of that. You wanted to stay home when the kids were born. You were the one who decided your friends lacked the status my friends had. Help me out here—I'm having trouble remembering your other sacrifices."

It was the wife's turn to be silent.

"All I wanted over the past few years was to hear you say 'thank you' like you did when we were first married. You were so grateful for every little thing I did. I haven't heard a word of gratitude from you in years." With that, he left the room as his wife tried to process the truth he had just spoken.

We can be like that wife in our relationship with God. We sacrifice for Him, giving up things we needed to be rid of anyway, being nice to people who know we're Christians when we'd rather make some snide remark to them, giving our money and our time to causes that we think will please God.

Meanwhile, what He wants from us is clear: He wants our praise and thanksgiving, which is actually so much easier for us to give! Stopping throughout the day to thank God for His gifts, His mercy, and His kindness is something that should come naturally to us. Gratitude is what pleases God, and there isn't a single thing we have to give up in order to express our thankfulness to Him.

Praise and glory and wisdom and thanks and honor and power
and strength be to our God for ever and ever.

REVELATION 7:12

The Payoff for Gratitude

"If the prayers of Christians were all to be noted for any one single day,
I fear it would be found that with them, as it was with the ten lepers
who had been cleansed, nine out of every ten had offered no genuine
thanks at all. Our Lord Himself was grieved at these ungrateful lepers
and said: 'Were there not ten cleansed? But where are the nine?
Were there not any found who returned to give glory to God
except this foreigner?' (Luke 17:17–18). Will He have
to ask the same question regarding any of us?"

The youth group at a small church had been invited to have
a private pool party at a local swimming club. The owner of
the facilities, a widow who attended a different church, had
enlisted the help of volunteers from her own church to provide
food and beverages for the party and keep an eye out for the
safety of the teenagers. The owner saw this event as a way
of promoting a sense of camaraderie among the churches in
town.

This first pool party was so successful that there was no
doubt youth groups from other churches would be invited to
have their own parties throughout the summer. As the party
drew to an end, most of the kids left. But a few stayed behind
and started helping the volunteers clean up. Not only did they

tell the volunteers to sit down and relax, they also thanked them and their hostess as well. They were the only ones who did.

Little did the teens know that their hostess was the mother of a backup singer for a popular recording artist, and she had a number of VIP tickets for the concert and a backstage meet and greet. Those teens had no idea that their kind gesture and thankful words would result in a payoff; they did and said what was in their hearts, and their grateful hostess wanted to acknowledge that in some way.

Our gestures and words of gratitude toward God need to be given in the same spirit. Imagine how much joy it brings Him when we thank Him from our heart, never even considering the possibility of anything in return. Few of us thank Him because we are genuinely grateful for all He has done for us, but those who do touch the very heart of God.

Just as you received Christ Jesus as Lord, continue to live your lives in him, rooted and built up in him, strengthened in the faith as you were taught, and overflowing with thankfulness.

COLOSSIANS 2:6–7

Stop All That Grumbling!

*"Some people are always complaining, nothing ever pleases them,
and no kindness seems ever to be appreciated. We know how
uncomfortable the company of such people makes us. How often
is it despairingly said of fretful, complaining spirits upon whom every
care and attention has been lavished, 'Will nothing ever satisfy them?'
And how often must God turn away, grieved by our complaining,
when His love has been lavished on us in untold blessings."*

It's a good thing for us that God has perfect patience. All through recorded time, He's had to put up with our grumbling. Just think of a few things people have complained about, often in the form of an accusatory question:

- Why don't You send rain to our drought-stricken land?
- Why do You continue to send rain to our flooded land?
- Why don't You ever answer my prayers?
- Why don't You ever answer my prayers the way I want You to?
- Why do the worst people seem to have the best stuff?
- Why do the best people seem to have the worst luck?

And so on. Fortunately, we have the assurance that He

will never give us what we deserve. In highly emphatic terms, He tells us that He will never leave us or abandon us; in fact, the original wording of that promise is so strong that it's as if He repeats it three times. *"This is it,"* He says. *"I'm not going anywhere. I am with you throughout eternity."*

The grace God has directed at us, however, was not intended to spoil us but to fill our hearts with gratitude and send us on our way to tell others of His great love and mercy. The Gospels tell us of an encounter Jesus had with nine lepers. He healed them all, which was no small thing for a leper. Not only were their bodies restored but their lives as well. Nine were healed, but only one came back to thank Him. What joy that one thankful heart must have brought Jesus. What encouragement for His tired feet and His voice strained from teaching the multitudes.

He has given us so much more than He gave those lepers. He restored their lives, but He has given us "eternal" life, and He did so without being asked and at indescribable cost to Himself. Can't we take time to turn and thank Him?

Through Jesus, therefore, let us continually offer to God a sacrifice of praise—the fruit of lips that openly profess his name.

HEBREWS 13:15

Gaining It All

*"If only we knew that the provision our divine Master has
made of spiritual drink and spiritual food is just what is best for us.
The amazing thing is that we cannot believe now, without waiting
for the end, that the Shepherd knows what pasture is best for His sheep.
Surely if we did, our hearts would be filled with thanksgiving
and our mouths with praise even in the wilderness."*

We live in such an astonishing age that nearly all of human knowledge can fit on a tiny microchip that most people have access to. Even though the technology is in its infancy, we've grown so accustomed to it that we barely give it a second thought anymore. If we want to know the average income of a family of six in a certain township in Zimbabwe, we can get that information in a few seconds. The full texts of much of the world's greatest literature can be downloaded with ease, just as we can view gallery after gallery of the world's greatest art any time we'd like.

There's a lot of information we can't find on the Internet, though, like what is best for us personally, in every aspect of our lives. How can we be sure we're in the right vocation? The Internet can provide career tests and guidance, but each of us is unique, and no personality or skills test can take into consideration our myriad facets. We have access to loads of information on healthy eating, but how can we find out exactly which nutrients we as individuals need and in exactly what quantity? We can't Google that and expect an accurate answer.

The only one who knows what is best for us is God, but it can be so hard for us to grasp the significance of that even when we think we understand it and believe it. How can we possibly believe that losing our house to foreclosure is what's best for us? Surely God had nothing to do with that. He only leads us into prosperous situations, right?

Not quite; He leads us toward what is best for us, and that could mean anywhere—including a place where we lose everything but gain even more in the end. If losing material possessions means gaining a deeper trust in God, then we've gained it all.

For his sake I have suffered the loss of all things,
and I regard them as rubbish, in order that I may gain Christ.

PHILIPPIANS 3:8 NRSV

Joy—or Sorrow?

"No depth of misery is too great for the sacrifice of thanksgiving. We cannot give thanks for the misery, but we can give thanks to the Lord in the misery. No matter what our trouble, the Lord is in it somewhere, and He is there to help and bless us. It is not because things are good that we are to thank the Lord, but because He is good. We are not wise enough to judge whether things are really, in their essence, joys or sorrows. But we always know that the Lord is good and that His goodness makes it absolutely certain that everything He provides or permits must be good."

Certainly we are wise enough to recognize that when something makes us happy, we can consider that to be a joy. Likewise, if something causes us to break down in tears, then we know to identify that as a sorrow. But is it possible to confuse the two?

Sometimes we think we know the whole story, but we only see a small fraction of what is actually going on. We're most vulnerable when it comes to our children. Their disappointments cause us seemingly interminable grief. Maybe our daughter wasn't accepted into the university she had her heart set on, and we lose sleep writing imaginary letters telling the administration what they've missed by rejecting her.

What we don't know is that her second-choice school, the

one that did accept her, is about to receive a large endowment for its International Studies Department—her chosen field. As an incoming freshman, she will have four years of overseas study opportunities that her counterparts at her first-choice university can only dream of. What appeared to be a sorrow was in fact a joy that had yet to be revealed.

A fly that has landed on intricately patterned wallpaper can see little of the design. But when it's seen from across the room, the overall design of the wallpaper becomes clear; patterns emerge and make sense in relation to each other. What we see of the circumstances of our lives is microscopic compared to God's all-knowing perspective. He sees the whole picture—how our situation affects *this* person, who responds to us in a way that affects *that* person, and so on.

When we finally get it—when we finally realize that God really does work everything together for good—we can relax, knowing that He is fitting our joys and our sorrows together into a beautiful, intricate design.

You will show me the path of life; in Your presence is fullness of joy; at Your right hand are pleasures forevermore.

PSALM 16:11 NKJV

Doorway to His Presence

"We are commanded to enter into His gates with thanksgiving and into His courts with praise, and I am convinced that the giving of thanks is the key that opens these gates more quickly than anything else. Try it, dear reader. The next time you feel dead, cold, and depressed, begin to praise and thank the Lord. Number the benefits He has bestowed on you, thank Him heartily for each one, and see if your spirits don't begin to rise and your heart get warmed up."

Doors are a great metaphor for the opportunities that open up to us as well as those that are closed to us. Just about everyone understands what an open or closed door symbolizes in art and literature, and we can often figure out which key opens a locked door. In romances, a faithful act may be the key that opens a heart locked up by the bitterness of betrayal. In mysteries, a vital but previously overlooked clue could be the key that opens the door to determining who the culprit is.

Doors—and gates—have a prominent place in one of the oldest surviving works of literature still in regular use, the Bible. What wonderful metaphors they are for entering into God's presence! The doorways to God's presence help us understand what's happening when we find it hard to sense that God is with us.

The problem is not that God isn't with us; it's that the door to His presence has been closed—from our side. The Bible doesn't say specifically what caused the door to close, but if we examine our lives, we could each determine what we've done to shut—and sometimes lock—the door that leads to God.

So how do we open the door to God? Prayer works, but when we're already far from God, behind a closed door, our prayers can become self-pitying, pleading attempts to get God to like us again. We imagine a problem that doesn't even exist—that God's love is fickle.

But when we take the focus off ourselves and place it on God through praise and adoration, suddenly the lock clicks, the door swings wide, and there we are, in the presence of the Creator of the universe. Praise and adoration are the keys that never get jammed and always grant us access to God's presence.

[Jesus said,] "Here I am! I stand at the door and knock.
If anyone hears my voice and opens the door, I will come in
and eat with that person, and they with me."

REVELATION 3:20

The Ultimate Hallelujah Chorus

"The last verse of the Book of Psalms, taken in connection with the vision of John in the book of Revelation, is very significant. The psalmist says, 'Let everything that has breath praise the LORD' (Psalm 150:6). And in the book of Revelation, John tells us that he heard this being done. 'And every creature which is in heaven and on the earth and under the earth and such as are in the sea, and all that are in them, I heard saying, "Blessing and honor and glory and power be to him who sits on the throne, and to the Lamb, forever and ever!"' (Revelation 5:13). The time for universal praise is sure to come some day. Let us begin to do our part now."

It's the biggest sports event of the year, and annually millions of people around the world tune in to watch it online and on television. They chant and shout, joining their voices with those of the thousands of fans in the stadium. The event is the Super Bowl, and if all those voices could be heard simultaneously, the noise would be deafening. All that just for a football game.

It's hard to imagine now, but a future event will create a sound that will put the Super Bowl to shame—when every living being will begin to praise God with their voices and continue praising Him throughout eternity. That's hard to imagine. We have no idea what it would be like to praise God forever.

When people are discouraged about the lack of honor that God is shown in our contemporary culture, we need to encourage them and give them hope by reminding them of the promise that one day, every person will bow down to God and acknowledge Him as Lord. That's when the awesome chorus of praise will begin. It will be a holy moment that will have no equal.

The prelude to that universal sound is playing right now, as each of us lifts our voices in praise to God, alone in our homes and with others in choirs and congregations around the world. We're all preparing for that wonderful day when we'll experience the greatest "Hallelujah Chorus" ever.

At the name of Jesus every knee should bend, in heaven and on earth and under the earth, and every tongue should confess that Jesus Christ is Lord, to the glory of God the Father.

PHILIPPIANS 2:10–11 NRSV

Every Human Heart

"God's ultimate purpose in our creation was that we should finally be 'conformed to the image of Christ.' Christ was to be the firstborn among many brethren, and His brethren were to be like Him. All the discipline and training of our lives is with this end in view, and God has implanted in every human heart a longing, however unformed and unexpressed, after the best and highest it knows."

The hero's quest is a mainstay of fiction and cinema. If the champion doesn't have something to strive for, we have little reason to pay attention to his story. In the "Bourne" books and movies, Jason Bourne seeks to unravel the mystery of his life and discover his true identity. In *The Hobbit*, Bilbo Baggins sets out to regain the dwarfs' treasure from the dragon Smaug. And boy meets girl in the search for a soul mate in every romance ever told.

Many quests aren't quite so noble, as when the goal is sexual fulfillment, the destruction of another culture, or murder. But some philosophers and theologians maintain that every human quest—not just the fictional ones—is a search for meaning, purpose, and ultimately a divine being, whether the seeker is aware of it or not.

Our own experiences bear this out. Whether we have

known God all our lives, found Him through an intentional search for spiritual truth, or turned to Him as a last resort when everything else in our lives had failed, we understand that longing to discover the reason we're here and the one who placed us here.

Though we often become dismayed when our loved ones don't seem to share our love of God, we know that every human heart has the same longing for Him. Some people never show it, while others never recognize it in themselves, but still, it's there.

This truth that every person is seeking God in some way should cause us to rejoice and never give up the hope that others will someday share our faith in God. When we begin to look at people with this knowledge always in our minds, our dismay will vanish into thin air.

"You will call on me and come and pray to me, and I will listen to you. You will seek me and find me when you seek me with all your heart."

JEREMIAH 29:12–13

Still in the Factory

"Our likeness to His image is an accomplished fact in the mind of God, but we are, so to speak, still in the factory, and the great master Workman is at work on us. 'It has not yet been revealed what we shall be, but we know that when He is revealed, we shall be like Him; for we shall see Him as He is' (1 John 3:2)."

$\mathcal{Y}$ears ago, a saying became popular among Christians, and it began showing up on posters and woodcarvings and other types of home decor. It was a simple truth, but it packed a powerful message: "Please be patient with me; God is not finished with me yet." Instead of providing an excuse for our behavior, for the most part it served as a much-needed reminder that we could not expect to be transformed into God's image overnight.

Could God accomplish that, though? Could He have made us like Him with a snap of His fingers? He could have. But what would that accomplish? We might think it would be a great idea if we could become like Him in the twinkling of an eye, but imagine the havoc that would wreak on the people around us. No matter how pleasant an instantaneous change may sound to us, we need to always remember that God knows what He's doing, and we don't. It's a humbling thought.

As we ask others to be patient with us while we're still in God's factory, we have to be patient with them as well. God is working on them, too, whether or not they realize it. Patience is one of the greatest qualities we can have, because it can have a radical effect on our relationships. But it is also one of the slowest to acquire; by its very nature, patience cannot be hastened. It involves slowing down, taking deep breaths, and thinking carefully before speaking or acting. That runs counter to our fast-paced way of living.

Being in God's factory is so wonderful because He can already see the final product; He knows what it means and what it looks like for us to be made in His image. It doesn't matter that we can't quite grasp that. We're living on a need-to-know basis in this life, and all we need to know is that the master Workman knows the final result.

You have stripped off the old self with its practices and have clothed yourselves with the new self, which is being renewed in knowledge according to the image of its creator.

COLOSSIANS 3:9–10 NRSV

Welcome the Process

"In view of such a glorious destiny, shall we not cheerfully welcome the processes, however painful they may be, by which we are to reach it? And shall we not strive eagerly and earnestly to be 'laborers together with God' in helping to bring it about? He is the great master Builder, but He wants our cooperation in building up the fabric of our characters, and He exhorts us to be careful how we build. All of us at every moment of our lives are engaged in this building. Sometimes we build with gold, silver, and precious stones, and sometimes we build with wood, hay, and stubble (see 1 Corinthians 3:12). And we are solemnly warned that every man's work is going to be revealed, 'for the Day will declare it, because it will be revealed by fire' (1 Corinthians 3:13)."

A severely obese man was given an ultimatum by each of his doctors—his general practitioner, a diabetes specialist, and a cardiologist—that if he didn't get serious about losing weight, he would die sooner rather than later. At forty-three, this was not what he wanted to hear, especially with three young children and a stay-at-home wife. He had been ignoring his doctors' advice for years, but with the possibility of death looming over him, he realized his lifestyle had to change. His family needed him.

He glanced at the first page of the treatment plan from the

diabetes doctor and silently said, "No way!" Salad? Fresh fruit and vegetables? Fish? Seriously? He was a meat and potatoes guy from as far back as he could remember. And that was just the dietary part of the plan. The second page covered the dreaded *e* word—exercise. Walk thirty minutes a day, three days a week, incrementally adding more time and more days.

But his wife came up with a plan of her own. She enlisted the help of their eleven-year-old daughter. She was the apple of his eye—and she agreed to walk with him when he got home from work and help her mother cook a nutritious meal for him on the nights when she didn't have too much homework.

The process of becoming more like Christ is never easy, but our love for God should be our primary motivation, just as a father's love for his daughter made his wife's plan work. When we allow God to work on us, we show our love for Him, as well as respect for His creation—us.

> *Don't copy the behavior and customs of this world,*
> *but let God transform you into a new person*
> *by changing the way you think.*

ROMANS 12:2 NLT

Seeing with Spiritual Eyes

"In order to be laborers with God, we must not only build with His materials but also by His processes. Our idea of building is of hard work done in the sweat of our brow, but God's idea is far different. Paul tells us what it is. 'We all,' he says, 'with unveiled face, beholding as in a mirror the glory of the Lord, are being transformed into the same image from glory to glory, just as by the Spirit of the Lord' (2 Corinthians 3:18). Our work is to 'behold,' and as we behold, the Lord effects the marvelous transformation, and we are changed into the same image by the Spirit of the Lord. This means, of course, to behold not in our earthly sense of merely looking at a thing, but in the divine sense of really seeing it."

What do we actually see when we look in a mirror? Do we see our thoughts, our values, our personality? Do we see what's going on deep inside us, the stirring of our spirit, our capacity for love, our wisdom? We don't see any of those things, because a physical mirror reflects only our physical attributes—hair and eye color, our facial expression, the nose we inherited from our father. A mirror cannot show us anything beyond the physical.

So what do we see when we look at God? If we see a physical image—a kindly old man with a long white beard sitting in the sky, a stern judge presiding over a courtroom, a king who dares not let anyone come near his gold-and-diamond encrusted throne—we have a major problem. God is spirit and can only be seen with spiritual sight, not with our physical eyes.

As we "behold" Him—as we focus our spiritual sight on Him—we begin to see the effects of His presence on us. We discover that we don't need to see Him physically, because our spiritual eyes have been opened to all that He is in our lives. We can see how we've gotten the better end of the deal. God has the task of handling a stubborn and relentlessly disobedient people. Our responsibility? It's to behold Him. In doing so, our hearts cannot help but become warm and malleable in His loving hands.

> *[Jesus said,] "A time is coming and has now come when the true worshipers will worship the Father in the Spirit and in truth, for they are the kind of worshipers the Father seeks."*
>
> JOHN 4:23

Judging by His Standards

"If we would be conformed to the image of Christ, then we must live closer and closer to Him. We must become better and better acquainted with His character and His ways; we must look at things through His eyes and judge all things by His standards."

The members of a midsized church were embroiled in a conflict over whether a sizable donation should be used for outreach to the poor or for sprucing up the church's exterior, which had seen better days. Splitting the donation and funding both projects was not possible because the donor had stipulated that all the money be used for one project only, hoping that the congregation would come to a consensus on their own.

In an effort to encourage the people to try to see the situation from God's perspective and seek His resolution to the problem, the pastor convened a church-wide meeting. Realizing that many still had a childlike impression of God looking down on them from the sky, he drew a triangle on a whiteboard, with the label "God" at the top, "Outreach" on the lower left angle, and "Building" on the lower right angle.

"Do you see what I'm getting at? God can see both perspectives at the same time from His vantage point. But neither side down here at the base can possibly have that same

perspective, considering where they're situated. They—you—
need to seek God's perspective and see the situation as He
sees it."

He hadn't gotten the point across to everyone, but the few
who did grasp it became instrumental in bringing the matter to
a close within a few weeks. Years later, one woman sought out
the pastor when health issues forced him to leave the area and
said, "That triangle illustration helped me learn to see things
from God's perspective and get over my childish way of seeing
God as 'up there'! I know now that He's everywhere, but still,
I'm grateful for the triangle!"

If a simple illustration can help us see things from God's
perspective, then so be it! We need to develop a mature faith,
and God can use whatever it takes to make that happen.
Maturity has many facets, but one is the ability to see things
from another person's perspective, and more importantly, from
God's perspective.

> *"As the heavens are higher than the earth, so are my ways higher*
> *than your ways and my thoughts than your thoughts."*
>
> ISAIAH 55:9

Christ Lives in Us

"Christ is to 'dwell in our hearts by faith,' and He can dwell there in no other way. Paul, when he tells us that he was crucified with Christ, says: 'It is no longer I who live, but Christ lives in me; and the life which I now live in the flesh I live by the faith in the Son of God, who loved me and gave himself for me' (Galatians 2:20). 'Christ lives in me,' this is the transforming secret. If Christ lives in me, His life must be revealed in my flesh, and I cannot fail to be changed from glory to glory into His image."

Medieval Christians were familiar with the "mysteries" of the faith. The Virgin Birth, the Resurrection, and the Trinity were some of the hallmarks of Christianity that people accepted by faith. They realized that this side of heaven they could never understand how a virgin could conceive a child and give birth, how a dead man could be raised alive from the grave, or how God the Father, God the Son, and God the Holy Spirit could be one God. They didn't understand, but they believed, and that was all that mattered.

Likewise, Christ living in us is another mystery of the faith. And yet all Christians believe this, whether or not they use the word *mystery* to describe it. We understand that Christ is spirit; we can sort of wrap our heads around that because we realize we have a spirit also. But does the fact that He lives in us mean that He is somehow contained in our bodies? How can He be, since one's spirit can't be contained?

It's easy to see how confusing this can be when we try to apply our limited human understanding to what is essentially a religious mystery. But we can understand that God has said that Christ dwells within each of us—and because God said it, we can take it as the gospel truth.

And if Christ truly lives in us, His life will be seen in ours. That will always be the true test of our commitment and desire to become more like Him.

God has chosen to make known among the Gentiles
the glorious riches of this mystery, which
is Christ in you, the hope of glory.

COLOSSIANS 1:27

"Sin must disappear at the incoming of Christ.
The 'old man' must be put off if the new man is to reign.
But both the putting off and the putting on must be done by faith.
There is no other way. We must move our personality, our ego,
our will out of self and into Christ. We must reckon ourselves
to be dead to self and alive only to God."

For most of her life, a college freshman considered herself to be strong in faith—a regular churchgoer, a leader among her teen peers in youth group, and an outspoken voice for morality. In college she met vibrant Christians who responded to God in an active way and seldom made a move of any importance without praying about it first, and she began attending their prayer meetings.

At her third meeting, she found the courage to speak up after they had prayed about hosting a free monthly dinner for the community. "Isn't that a no-brainer?" she asked. "Let's just do it!"

One guy said they felt they should pray about things that weren't clear-cut and that involved money. Later they prayed about sponsoring a concert featuring a contemporary Christian band.

"It seems like we should just do these things," she whispered to a girl sitting next to her.

After the meeting the girl took her aside. "Here's the thing. We need to get out of the way and find out what God wants us to do, not what we want to do. He knows whether the dinner or the concert will be a wise use of our time and money. We have to move over and let Him in." That night, the freshman's life with God began to change in a radical way.

Getting rid of phrases like "But I want. . ." and "But I think. . ." is a start at becoming transformed to God's image, because those words express the desires of our own ego and will. As we become more accustomed to discovering what God wants us to do and what God thinks about a certain situation, we demonstrate that we are actively working to get our old nature out of the way so the miracle of transformation can occur.

Christians call this "dying" to self, which would sound morbid if it wasn't such a wonderful thing to do. When we die to self, we move over and allow Christ in. That's when we become fully alive—alive to Christ.

Count yourselves dead to sin but alive to God in Christ Jesus.

ROMANS 6:11

Real Regeneration

"Faith calls those things that don't exist as though they do, and, in so calling them, brings them into being. Therefore, although we cannot see any tangible sign of change when by faith we put off the old man and by faith put on the new man, yet it has really been done, and faith has accomplished it. Those souls who abandon the self-life and give themselves up to the Lord to be fully possessed by Him find that He takes possession of their being and works there to will and to do of His good pleasure."

$\mathcal{A}$ well-known "fact" is that the cells in the human body regenerate every seven years. But this so-called fact isn't true. Some cells regenerate every few days, some much less frequently than every seven years, and some never at all. But it is true that throughout our lifetimes, most of our cells are renewed, and by the time we die, we really are almost entirely new people.

What's astonishing is that all this happens inside us without us feeling a thing. Our cells die and are restored, and we go on eating our ham sandwich and drinking our diet soda and generally being bored with our day as if nothing amazing is happening to us. If we can't see it, feel it, hear it, smell it, or taste it, there's nothing going on, right?

Wrong. Just as our cells regenerate, our spirit regenerates

when we have Christ living inside us and through us. Day by day, we are changed into His likeness, whether we can sense it or not. We can't help it; the more we give ourselves over to Him, the more we become like Him. The only way we can block that transformation is by pushing Him aside and allowing our old nature—our selfish desires and stubborn will—to take His place.

For a time, popular media was obsessed with demonic possession, the notion that demons can take over and possess our spirits. But what about godly possession? When we allow Jesus to take over our lives, we become God possessed. We willingly and joyfully cede ownership to Him, and that begins the process of regeneration, renewal, and transformation. Our lives are no longer our own—thank God!—and we become His. Could there be any better reason to kick the old nature to the curb and invite God in?

Not by works of righteousness which we have done,
but according to [God's] mercy he saved us, by the washing
of regeneration, and renewing of the Holy Ghost.

TITUS 3:5 KJV

A Glimpse of Christ

*"We will not be fully changed into the image of Christ until He appears,
but meanwhile, the life of Jesus is 'revealed in our flesh.'
Is it revealed in ours? Are we so 'conformed to the image'
of Christ that men see in us a glimpse of Him?
Is it obvious to all around us that we have been with Jesus?"*

*A*h! I see you've been with Jesus!"

The young man could hardly believe his ears. He hadn't seen his grandfather for six months, but in the meantime, so much had happened. His girlfriend shared how Jesus had changed her life and encouraged him to start reading the New Testament. He had spent a lot of time reading classic Christian works by writers dating back to the third century. Early on, he became convinced that Jesus was who He said He was.

"Grandpop, how did you know?" he asked in astonishment.

His grandfather chuckled. "Look at you—you're alive with joy! I would have thought you were in love, but this is a different kind of love, isn't it?"

His grandfather was right. He and his girlfriend had decided they weren't right for each other but had remained friends. There was no new girl in his life.

"Son, you've changed," the older man said. "You called to see if you could come stay with me for a while. You've never done that. I know you used to call me a Jesus freak"—he held up his hand to keep his grandson from interrupting—"and that was okay, because even though you meant it as an insult, I wore it as a badge of honor. But when you called, there was something different in your voice, a tenderness—you used to act so tough!

"Your grandmother and I prayed for you every day before she died, and I kept it up since then. When I opened the door to you just now and you hugged me and told me you loved me, well, it was obvious. Only Jesus could account for that kind of change."

If we have been spending quality time with God, paying attention to who He is and what He has to say to us, people will take notice. Other Christians will know to give the credit to God, but even those people who don't have a relationship with God will recognize something different about us— something good. It's inevitable. When we cooperate with God, transformation follows.

[The LORD] guides the humble in what is right and teaches them his way.

PSALM 25:9

181

Revealing Who We Are

"Paul says we are to be 'epistles of Christ,' known and read of all men, 'written not with ink but by the Spirit of the living God, not on tablets of stone but on tablets of flesh, that is, of the heart' (Ephesians 3:2–3). If every child of God would begin from this day forward to be an 'epistle of Christ,' living a truly Christlike life, it would not be a month before the churches would all be crowded with inquirers, coming in to see what was the religion that could so transform human nature into something divine. We must meet unbelievers with transformed lives."

After being elected class flirt in her high school popularity contest, a senior realized that her newfound notoriety wasn't all she thought it would be. She had always considered her flirtations to be innocent fun, especially since she was a member of an after-school Bible club and her church's choir. She figured no one would take her behavior seriously.

But suddenly, she was in high demand among the guys in the school. Once her cell number started making the rounds, she was receiving texts from a few guys she knew and a lot she didn't. Her guy friends mostly just teased her about her popularity, but the ones she didn't know asked when they could get together with her. At first she was mildly flattered, but soon enough the texts became more and more suggestive. After receiving a lewd photo on her phone, she broke down crying and called her best friend, who decided it was time to share some hard truths with her friend.

"Look, I know you thought this whole flirting thing was fun, but a lot of guys have a different definition of 'fun.' "

"But I'm a Christian! How could they think I would do that?"

"How would they know you're a Christian when you act like you're not?"

That's a question we all need to ask ourselves. Maybe we are still friends with people we socialized with before we got serious about our relationship with God, and that's fine— unless we purposely resist showing them who we are now. That doesn't mean we have to always talk about God or act as if we're somehow better. It means that we no longer join in when they're gossiping or making fun of others. It means that we're real with them, revealing who we are today—a person transformed by the love of God.

Be an example to the believers with your words,
your actions, your love, your faith, and your pure life.

1 TIMOTHY 4:12 NCV

Not for Display Only

"It is very easy to have a church religion or a prayer meeting religion or a Christian-work religion, but it is altogether a different thing to have an everyday religion. To show godly character at home is one of the most vital parts of Christianity, but it is also one far too rare; and it is not at all an uncommon thing to find Christians who 'do their righteousness' before outsiders 'to be seen of men,' but who fail miserably in showing Christlike character at home."

When a deacon's wife made an appointment for a counseling session with her pastor, she made a special request that his wife attend the session as well. It was an unusual but not unheard-of request, and the pastoral couple agreed to conduct the meeting together.

"I know you think the world of my husband, and I know he has served the church well," the woman said, keeping her eyes on her pastor. "But he's a different man at home, and I don't know how much more of his controlling, holier-than-thou attitude I can take. I want to leave him."

The pastor was shocked. They seemed to be the perfect couple—young but dedicated to God, always ready to help out, faithful in attendance. And he was a deacon! Everyone looked up to him. Everything in him told this pastor that the woman was either exaggerating or lying; maybe she had another reason for wanting to leave. He started to grill her, but his wife touched his hand—their private signal that meant "stop."

"I've noticed his behavior when I've stopped by to visit you," the pastor's wife said to the woman. "He's subtle when I'm there, but I believe you. Let's talk about how we can change this situation."

It's so hard to believe that the people we admire for their godly behavior in public can be so ungodly at home. Yet we've all heard of stories about celebrated Christian leaders, both male and female, who betray, berate, or lash out at their families. We don't hear as many stories about laypeople doing the same, but that's only because they aren't well-known.

With the divorce rate among Christians nearly equaling that of secular couples, it's evident that some aren't acting in a Christlike way in the home. Our faith was never intended to be used "for display only"; it is to be actively lived out in the most difficult place ever, within our own homes.

He who walks with integrity walks securely,
but he who perverts his ways will become known.

PROVERBS 10:9 NKJV

*"What we do to be seen of men is seen of men, and that is all there
is to it. There is no conformity to the image of Christ in this sort of
righteousness. To bear everyday trials cheerfully and be patient under home
provocations; to return good for evil and meet the frictions of daily life with
sweetness and gentleness; to suffer long and be kind; to not envy or flaunt
oneself; to not be puffed up or seek one's own; to not be easily provoked; to
think no evil; bear all things, believe all things, hope all things, endure all
things—this is what it means to be conformed to the image of Christ!
Do we know anything of such righteousness as this?"*

It's a rare Christian who hasn't wished they could do
something magnificent for God. We want to be the one who
follows in the footsteps of the world's great evangelists and
bring thousands, if not millions, to Christ. Or maybe it's our
fervent desire to leave the trappings of American culture
behind, travel to an emerging nation, and be the first to really
get through to the people with the truth of the Gospel. If
we can't do either of those things, then maybe we could be
a singer in a praise band that performs at megachurches,
religious festivals, and concert venues across the country.

As glorious as those options may sound, our task is to be
conformed to the image of Christ, right where we are. We're

the mass of unknowns, those who will never receive public accolades for our great faith in God. But living out our faith in everyday circumstances can have a greater impact on others than we'll ever know. Better yet, we'll be living out our faith in simple obedience to God.

Every time we treat with kindness a person who has done us great harm, we become more like Christ. Every time we graciously step back so another may enjoy the spotlight, we become more conformed to His image. And every time we patiently resist the urge to return an insult to an insulting person who may simply be having a bad day, we come closer to having the mind of Christ.

Becoming more like Christ is our job, whether we're on a stage before thousands of people or an audience of one. Please Him, and we've won it all.

We take thought beforehand and aim to be honest and absolutely above suspicion, not only in the sight of the Lord but also in the sight of men.

2 CORINTHIANS 8:21 AMP

Charity That Matters

"Some Christians seem to think that the fruits that the Bible calls for are some form of outward religious work, such as holding meetings, visiting the poor, running charitable institutions, and so forth. But the fact is that the Bible scarcely mentions these at all as fruits of the Spirit but declares that the fruit of the Spirit is love, joy, peace, long-suffering, gentleness, goodness, faith, meekness, temperance. A Christlike character must necessarily be the fruit of Christ's indwelling. Other things will no doubt be the outcome of this character; but first and foremost comes the character, or all the rest is but a hollow sham."

The nineteenth century was a time of great social upheaval, in both Europe and North America. In urban areas in particular, the chasm between the haves and the have-nots was especially evident. The elegant houses, mansions, and estates of the wealthy stood in stark contrast to the lice- and rodent-infested slums where the infirm, disabled, and unemployed lived alongside the working poor. Conditions were so deplorable that for the most part, civic authorities looked away.

But one segment of society could not look away—the Christians who took seriously Christ's admonition that the way we treat the "least" among us is the way we treat Christ Himself. Hospitals, hospices, soup kitchens, food and clothing distribution centers, and homeless shelters began cropping up in the slums, frequently run by Christian women who volunteered their time and services. Eventually, girls' schools were also established so young women would have an opportunity for employment.

History records these monumental achievements, but a record of the character of the women and men who sacrificed their own comfort for the sake of those who had next to nothing is lost to us. Were these people do-gooders expecting to earn points with God, or were these acts of charity the result of a deep relationship with God among people who knew and believed that the two great commandments were to love God and to love others?

People on the receiving end of charity aren't especially interested in the motivation of those who provide it, but God is. He doesn't keep score by tallying up the number of good works we do. He looks at our hearts. Are our hearts turned toward Him? Do we genuinely love Him and our neighbors? If we serve our neighbors as a result of that love, well, that's all the better.

Though I am free and belong to no one, I have made myself
a slave to everyone, to win as many as possible.

1 CORINTHIANS 9:19

We're All Unfinished

"It is to be by His working in us that this purpose of God in our creation is to be accomplished. If it should look like some of us are too far removed from any conformity to the image of Christ for such a transformation to ever happen, we must remember that our Maker is not finished making us yet. The day will come, if we do not hinder it, when the work begun in Genesis will be finished in Revelation."

To look at the guy at the end of the bar, few people would think that there was a soft heart beating inside such a hard-living man. Worn down and worn out from decades of physical labor, six-pack nights, and four failed marriages, he looked every bit the part of a weathered alcoholic for whom there was no hope. But anyone making that assumption would be wrong.

The drink on the bar in front of him was a nonalcoholic beer, his beverage of choice now that he was well into his seventh month of sobriety. His drinking buddies—he knew better than to consider them friends—had a running pool going, betting on when he'd fall off the wagon. Maybe hanging out at the bar wasn't such a good idea, but the people there were the only family he had, even though he wasn't related to any of them. The bartender was the closest thing he had to a real friend; he kept an eye out for him, made sure he had his favorite nonalcoholic beer in stock at all times, and even tolerated his occasional talk about God.

Although it was hard to convince some people that he'd changed, in time, he figured they'd catch on, just as the bartender had. He knew he didn't have long for this world, but in whatever time he had left, he would keep the promise he had made to God seven months earlier—he would arrive in heaven clean and sober, even if nobody but God knew it.

We must never forget that God is at work in every person's life in ways we cannot see. That guy who looks like a broken-down drunk? God is at work on his transformation. We should be glad that He is, because that means He's far from giving up on us, too!

The LORD does not look at the things people look at.
People look at the outward appearance, but the LORD looks at the heart.

1 SAMUEL 16:7

No Words Needed

"The last and greatest lesson that the soul has to learn is the fact that God, and God alone, is enough for all its needs. This is the lesson that all His dealings with us are meant to teach."

"Wait silently for God alone"—what does it mean to do that? How *can* we do that? If we break that admonition down word by word, we can see all too clearly why it is so hard to follow— but maybe we can gain some insight into how we can benefit from it, regardless of its difficulty.

"Wait"—most of us really dislike that word. We want what we want *now*. That's not always a bad thing, especially if our wants are tied to seeing something good come about in another person's life. In other words, wanting a Big Mac *now*—not so honorable a desire. Wanting to see a terminal patient come to Christ *now*—much better. But still, God exists in eternity, and it may seem like an eternity before we get what we want, if ever. Waiting gives us time to mature in our faith.

"Silently": Even harder! We want to shout and tell God to hurry as we're waiting! But silence offers a rare opportunity— the chance to settle our minds and our spirits so we can finally hear God. This is a *good* thing.

"For God": That's the root of this admonition. We are to

wait silently for *God*—not for an answer, not for a miracle, not for an activity or event. We must wait for Him. However long that takes, however painful the wait may be, we must not take a situation back into our own hands.

"Alone": Not God plus a reward, not God plus a blessing, not God plus *anything*. We must wait silently for Him alone. No one else, nothing else will come to our aid. It's God alone—no more and no less.

Those words express the all-sufficiency of God. We must place our trust in nothing else and nothing less than God alone—as we patiently wait without saying a word, because words aren't needed.

My soul, wait silently for God alone, for my expectation is from Him.
He only is my rock and my salvation; He is my defense;
I shall not be moved. In God is my salvation and my glory;
the rock of my strength, and my refuge, is in God.

PSALM 62:5–7 NKJV

Seeking Rest

"If God is indeed the 'God of all comfort'; if He is our Shepherd; if He is really and truly our Father; if, in short, all the many aspects we have been studying of His character and His ways are actually true, then we must come to the positive conviction that He is, in Himself alone, enough for all our possible needs, and that we may safely rest in Him absolutely and forever."

$\mathcal{R}$est is such a rare commodity in our culture that it's been suggested that our beds have become like another human being to us, taking on a distinct personality and acting like a magnet the way a romantic partner used to attract us. Sound crazy? Spend a half hour looking at ads for luxury hotels or bedding retailers, and such a notion won't seem so bizarre. The beds are piled high with downy comforters and soft, plush pillows; everything about the image says, "Ahhhh." The advertisers are selling *comfort*; they are well aware that at the end of a long, hard day—or even a short, easy day—what people want most of all is to stretch out in bed and fully relax.

But all that luxury bedding won't still our minds when they're churning with the troublesome events of the day. Our thoughts don't turn off automatically when our skin comes in contact with six-hundred-thread-count, Egyptian cotton sheets.

As a source of mental stress relief, luxury linens don't quite cut it. Those down pillows provide rest for our heads only; if they could rest our minds, what a miracle product they would be!

Many of us fail to realize that at the end of a long, hard day, or any other kind of day, we have access to the ultimate stress reliever, God Himself, the God of all comfort. So many images of God speak to His rest-giving nature: He's the Shepherd who makes us lie down in green pastures. He's the Father who made provision for us to enter into His eternal rest, His place of comfort for us. He's the Mother who nurtures us and attends to our every need. God keeps us safe in His presence.

How can we ever doubt that He loves us and cares for us? He has provided for us in every way possible, even in ways we cannot see. He is enough. He is more than enough. We can finally find rest, just knowing that.

Let the beloved of the LORD rest secure in him,
for he shields him all day long, and the one the LORD
loves rests between his shoulders.

DEUTERONOMY 33:12

One Foundation Will Stand

"No soul can be really at rest until it has given up all dependence on everything else and has been forced to depend on the Lord alone. As long as our expectation is from other things, nothing but disappointment awaits us. Feelings may change; doctrines and dogmas may be upset; Christian work may come to nothing; prayers may seem to lose their fervency; promises may seem to fail; everything that we have believed in or depended upon may seem to be swept away, and only God is left."

An older professor at a state university was highly regarded as a theological scholar, particularly concerning the doctrinal beliefs of a variety of Christian denominations in the United States. Often called upon to present papers at Christian colleges as well, the professor personally adhered to the basic doctrines of the church, but like many Christians, he had some cherished beliefs that only a few denominations shared. Given that there are thousands of Christian denominations, doctrines that are subject to interpretation or preference tend to find acceptance in some churches but not in others.

This scholar, however, had staked his professional reputation on his conclusion that the denomination he belonged to was *right*, in both practice and belief. Didn't the ancient texts support what his church believed about the standards for membership with regard to appropriate attire and what was forbidden on the Sabbath?

When a colleague challenged the professor on the flaws in his research, he spent months trying unsuccessfully to disprove him. When he realized he couldn't, he felt he had lost everything he had based his life and his career on. He had to rebuild his faith and his reputation, both of which had been founded not on Christ but on doctrines of secondary importance. After realizing that all he had left to depend on was God, he realized God was all he needed.

If the worldwide Christian church was built on God alone, what a different church we would have! Instead of thousands of denominations, we would be united in our love for God and our love for each other. But that's exactly what is going to happen someday, and we can start getting used to that way of life now, by making sure that our faith is built on God alone—the only foundation that will stand through eternity.

You are the body of Christ, and each one of you is a part of it.

1 CORINTHIANS 12:27

The One Who Promises

"We say sometimes, 'If I could only find a promise to fit my case,
I could then be at rest.' But promises may be misunderstood or misapplied,
and, at the moment when we are leaning all our weight on them,
they may seem utterly to fail us. But the Promiser, who is behind His
promises, can never fail nor change. The little child does not need to have
any promises from its mother to make it content; it has its mother herself,
and she is enough. Its mother is better than a thousand promises.
And should every promise be wiped out of the Bible,
we would still have God left, and God would be enough."

There's a malady that's common to most Christians, and it usually strikes in the early years of our newfound or renewed relationship with God. Let's call it "promisitis" for the sake of brevity. It's a flare-up of our assumed need to find a promise in the Bible that fits every situation in our lives, and it's a disease that's fraught with danger.

Take the case of a young woman who diligently read every verse in the Bible related to marriage as she tried to determine whether she should accept her boyfriend's proposal. She was a new Christian, and more than anything in the world, she wanted her boyfriend to also come to faith in Christ.

Aha! She finally found it—a verse in the book of Hosea

that assured Hosea's "lady" that she would come to know God if only she would marry him. What could be clearer? Accept her boyfriend's proposal, and then *he* will come to know God. But a closer look at the context reveals that the "lady" in Hosea's story was a prostitute who symbolized the nation of Israel, who had proved their unfaithfulness to God by worshipping idols.

While many promises in the Bible can be taken at face value, some are metaphors like the one in Hosea, and others apply only to circumstances specific to the place and time in which they were written. Still others are baffling and subject to interpretation.

But one thing that's clear is the character of the one who made those promises. He is faithful and He fully understands those things that bewilder us. It's God we need to place our trust in. Then we will recognize His promises as they are quickened to our hearts by the Holy Spirit and fulfilled in our lives.

The LORD is trustworthy in all he promises and faithful in all he does.

PSALM 145:13

Taking the High Road

*"We are to find God sufficient for all our spiritual needs,
whether we feel ourselves to be in a desert or in a fertile valley.
We are to say with the prophet: 'Though the fig tree may not blossom,
nor fruit be on the vines; though the labor of the olive may fail, and the
fields yield no food; though the flock may be cut off from the fold, and there
be no herd in the stall—yet I will rejoice in the LORD, I will joy in the God
of my salvation' (Habakkuk 3:17–18). The soul can never find rest short
of this. All God's dealings with us, therefore, are shaped to this end,
and He is often obliged to deprive us of all joy in everything else in
order that He may force us to find our joy only in Himself."*

One Idaho family built their dream house on a one-acre tract among similar homes deep in the wilderness. They loved the sound of the wind whistling through the fir trees at night and the way the sunlight flickered through the branches during the day. They were living their ideal life until the day they received a call that sounded the alarm—wildfire!

They had fifteen minutes to pack up and leave, because the winds they had once enjoyed were spreading the fire rapidly. Within an hour, everything they owned, except what little they were able to grab in their panic, was gone.

A year later, they had built a house in the safety of the

town—once again, among a stand of trees—and were starting to rebuild their lives when another fire whipped through the area, took an unexpected turn, and destroyed the family's new home in town, along with dozens of others.

The cynical among us might have a lot to say about this: Where was God? Why did they build again where there were trees? What kind of curse are they under? But this family took the high road, the one that led to the presence of God. There, they discovered that they had not lost anything worth holding on to. Today, they can even laugh—a little—about the times when God cleared their land just so He could get their attention. Far from blaming God, they give Him the credit— first, for rescuing them and keeping them safe, and second, for giving them eyes to see what really matters. Could we do the same?

As servants of God we commend ourselves in every way: . . .poor, yet making many rich; having nothing, and yet possessing everything.

2 CORINTHIANS 6:4, 10

God Is the Answer

*"If we want to see God, our interior questioning must be,
not about ourselves, but about Him. How does God feel toward me?
Is His love for me warm enough? Has He enough zeal?
Does He feel my need deeply enough? Is He sufficiently in earnest?
Although these questions may seem irreverent to some, they simply
embody the doubts and fears of many doubting hearts, and they only
need to be asked to prove the fact that these doubts and fears are in
themselves the real irreverence. We all know what would be the triumphant
answers to such questions. No doubts could withstand their testimony;
and the soul that asks and answers them honestly will know
the profound and absolute conviction that God is enough."*

In the 1960s, one frequently heard slogan among the
counterculture movement was "Question Everything," largely
because antiwar activists believed the information coming out
of the Vietnam conflict was highly suspect. Long after the
movement had lost its steam, some activists continued to live by
the slogan.

One such person was a young woman who gave up her
love beads for the love of Jesus. A convert to Christ during
the Jesus Movement of the 1970s, she returned to her loving
and ever-supportive family in Nebraska. The transition was

far from smooth, however, and one day the young woman's "Question Everything" philosophy surfaced. Things she had heard in church troubled her. She believed in Jesus and trusted Him with her life, but much of what she read in the Bible and heard in sermons didn't make sense and was hard to believe. She listed one thing after another that she had doubts about, including whether she was dishonoring God by having those doubts.

At first her mother was defensive, but soon she sensed God calming her spirit and was able to respond out of love for her daughter. "Honey, questioning anything will lead you to the answers if you pursue them," she said. "Talk to God about your doubts—He wants to lead you to the truth. He won't turn you away."

He won't turn us away either. We can't hide our questions from God; He knows the reason behind every doubt that keeps us from giving ourselves to Him entirely. When we choose to become transparent in His presence, we will discover that God Himself *is* the answer to all our questions, doubts, and fears.

What if some were unfaithful?
Will their unfaithfulness nullify God's faithfulness?
Not at all!

ROMANS 3:3–4

Claiming Our Inheritance

"It would be impossible for any statement to be more all-embracing. All things are yours because you belong to Christ. All things we need are part of our inheritance in Him, and they only await our claiming. Let our needs and difficulties be as great as they may, there is in these 'all things' a supply exceedingly abundantly above all we can ask or think."

A sixty-five-year-old woman was facing a mountain of decisions. Recently widowed, she would now have to learn to live on Social Security and choose from among the confusing Medicare options. Neither she nor her husband had been high earners during their working lives, and the little money her husband left to her was just enough for a modest funeral for him.

Just when things looked as if they couldn't get worse, a lawyer called and asked her to meet him at his office. During their meeting, the lawyer told the widow that one of her aunts had left her an inheritance of a quarter of a million dollars. But the widow objected; her family had not been close, and she had never heard of this aunt who supposedly left her some money. This had to be a scam, she said.

The lawyer managed to hide his astonishment, but he had never experienced anything like this. How could this be a scam? She was *getting* money, not being asked to give it! He spent the next half hour explaining the situation to her, both how inheritance law worked in their state and what it would mean to her life if she accepted the money.

The widow was so suspicious that she refused to claim her inheritance. She lived out the last years of her life in a sketchy rooming house with even sketchier tenants, while her inheritance was turned over to the state since she had no heirs.

It's hard to imagine anyone being so foolish, but every day, people walk away from the most amazing inheritance anyone could ever receive—everything God offers them. Compared to the riches of God's kingdom, a quarter of a million dollars is a mere drop in the bucket.

There's no need for suspicion; the inheritance is ours to claim. There's no scam involved; the Creator of the universe backs it up with His Word. All that He has promised us is rightfully ours—right here, right now.

"All things are yours, whether Paul or Apollos or Cephas or the world or life or death or the present or the future—all are yours, and you are of Christ, and Christ is of God."

1 Corinthians 3:21–23

No Begging Needed

"Nothing can separate you from God's love, absolutely nothing.
Can we not understand that God, who is love, who is, if I may say so,
made out of love, simply cannot help blessing us. We do not need to beg
Him to bless us—He simply cannot help it. Therefore God is enough!
God is enough for time; God is enough for eternity. God is enough!"

The fact that God speaks of His blessings as an inheritance is significant, because it means that in addition to the blessing itself, we also receive it without having to plead for it. It's not like the lottery, through which money is given only to a few people who happen to have chosen the right combination of numbers. Nor is it like bingo, where rewards are handed out to the first to reach the coveted five-in-a-row mark.

Our inheritance from God works like any other inheritance, with a few exceptions. It's like a human inheritance in that it is passed on to those whom the owner of the estate chooses—and God chooses to pass it along to His daughters and sons. We don't have to beg Him for it; it's ours, plain and simple. All we have to do is claim it.

It's different from human inheritance in significant ways, though. First, we don't have to split it with other heirs. That's hard to imagine because we think in finite terms. But God's supply is infinite, and there's no splitting involved. Second, our inheritance is incontestable. No one can deny us our right to claim it. Third, there's no human intermediary. We don't have to go to a lawyer's office for the reading of the will; we already know what's in it because the terms are spelled out in the Bible. Nor do we have to wait for the estate to be settled before we get our inheritance; it was settled when Jesus was crucified on Calvary.

So what are we waiting for? Since the estate was settled two millennia ago, doesn't that mean we have access to our inheritance now? We only need to claim that inheritance for our own and begin to live as heirs of God. And that means living a life of abundant love, joy, peace, patience, kindness, goodness, faithfulness, gentleness, and self-control.

How can we be sure of that? The God of all comfort has promised it.

Giving thanks unto the Father, which hath made us meet to be partakers of the inheritance of the saints in light: who hath delivered us from the power of darkness, and hath translated us into the kingdom of his dear Son.

COLOSSIANS 1:12–13 KJV

Scripture Index

Old Testament

New Testament

READ THRU THE BIBLE IN A YEAR

1-Jan	Gen. 1-2	Matt. 1	Ps. 1
2-Jan	Gen. 3-4	Matt. 2	Ps. 2
3-Jan	Gen. 5-7	Matt. 3	Ps. 3
4-Jan	Gen. 8-10	Matt. 4	Ps. 4
5-Jan	Gen. 11-13	Matt. 5:1-20	Ps. 5
6-Jan	Gen. 14-16	Matt. 5:21-48	Ps. 6
7-Jan	Gen. 17-18	Matt. 6:1-18	Ps. 7
8-Jan	Gen. 19-20	Matt. 6:19-34	Ps. 8
9-Jan	Gen. 21-23	Matt. 7:1-11	Ps. 9:1-8
10-Jan	Gen. 24	Matt. 7:12-29	Ps. 9:9-20
11-Jan	Gen. 25-26	Matt. 8:1-17	Ps. 10:1-11
12-Jan	Gen. 27:1-28:9	Matt. 8:18-34	Ps. 10:12-18
13-Jan	Gen. 28:10-29:35	Matt. 9	Ps. 11
14-Jan	Gen. 30:1-31:21	Matt. 10:1-15	Ps. 12
15-Jan	Gen. 31:22-32:21	Matt. 10:16-36	Ps. 13
16-Jan	Gen. 32:22-34:31	Matt. 10:37-11:6	Ps. 14
17-Jan	Gen. 35-36	Matt. 11:7-24	Ps. 15
18-Jan	Gen. 37-38	Matt. 11:25-30	Ps. 16
19-Jan	Gen. 39-40	Matt. 12:1-29	Ps. 17
20-Jan	Gen. 41	Matt. 12:30-50	Ps. 18:1-15
21-Jan	Gen. 42-43	Matt. 13:1-9	Ps. 18:16-29
22-Jan	Gen. 44-45	Matt. 13:10-23	Ps. 18:30-50
23-Jan	Gen. 46:1-47:26	Matt. 13:24-43	Ps. 19
24-Jan	Gen. 47:27-49:28	Matt. 13:44-58	Ps. 20
25-Jan	Gen. 49:29-Exod. 1:22	Matt. 14	Ps. 21
26-Jan	Exod. 2-3	Matt. 15:1-28	Ps. 22:1-21
27-Jan	Exod. 4:1-5:21	Matt. 15:29-16:12	Ps. 22:22-31
28-Jan	Exod. 5:22-7:24	Matt. 16:13-28	Ps. 23
29-Jan	Exod. 7:25-9:35	Matt. 17:1-9	Ps. 24
30-Jan	Exod. 10-11	Matt. 17:10-27	Ps. 25
31-Jan	Exod. 12	Matt. 18:1-20	Ps. 26
1-Feb	Exod. 13-14	Matt. 18:21-35	Ps. 27
2-Feb	Exod. 15-16	Matt. 19:1-15	Ps. 28
3-Feb	Exod. 17-19	Matt. 19:16-30	Ps. 29
4-Feb	Exod. 20-21	Matt. 20:1-19	Ps. 30
5-Feb	Exod. 22-23	Matt. 20:20-34	Ps. 31:1-8
6-Feb	Exod. 24-25	Matt. 21:1-27	Ps. 31:9-18
7-Feb	Exod 26-27	Matt. 21:28-46	Ps. 31:19-24
8-Feb	Exod. 28	Matt. 22	Ps. 32
9-Feb	Exod. 29	Matt. 23:1-36	Ps. 33:1-12

10-Feb	Exod. 30-31	Matt. 23:37-24:28	Ps. 33:13-22
11-Feb	Exod. 32-33	Matt. 24:29-51	Ps. 34:1-7
12-Feb	Exod. 34:1-35:29	Matt. 25:1-13	Ps. 34:8-22
13-Feb	Exod. 35:30-37:29	Matt. 25:14-30	Ps. 35:1-8
14-Feb	Exod. 38-39	Matt. 25:31-46	Ps. 35:9-17
15-Feb	Exod. 40	Matt. 26:1-35	Ps. 35:18-28
16-Feb	Lev. 1-3	Matt. 26:36-68	Ps. 36:1-6
17-Feb	Lev. 4:1-5:13	Matt. 26:69-27:26	Ps. 36:7-12
18-Feb	Lev. 5:14 -7:21	Matt. 27:27-50	Ps. 37:1-6
19-Feb	Lev. 7:22-8:36	Matt. 27:51-66	Ps. 37:7-26
20-Feb	Lev. 9-10	Matt. 28	Ps. 37:27-40
21-Feb	Lev. 11-12	Mark 1:1-28	Ps. 38
22-Feb	Lev. 13	Mark 1:29-39	Ps. 39
23-Feb	Lev. 14	Mark 1:40-2:12	Ps. 40:1-8
24-Feb	Lev. 15	Mark 2:13-3:35	Ps. 40:9-17
25-Feb	Lev. 16-17	Mark 4:1-20	Ps. 41:1-4
26-Feb	Lev. 18-19	Mark 4:21-41	Ps. 41:5-13
27-Feb	Lev. 20	Mark 5	Ps. 42-43
28-Feb	Lev. 21-22	Mark 6:1-13	Ps. 44
1-Mar	Lev. 23-24	Mark 6:14-29	Ps. 45:1-5
2-Mar	Lev. 25	Mark 6:30-56	Ps. 45:6-12
3-Mar	Lev. 26	Mark 7	Ps. 45:13-17
4-Mar	Lev. 27	Mark 8	Ps. 46
5-Mar	Num. 1-2	Mark 9:1-13	Ps. 47
6-Mar	Num. 3	Mark 9:14-50	Ps. 48:1-8
7-Mar	Num. 4	Mark 10:1-34	Ps. 48:9-14
8-Mar	Num. 5:1-6:21	Mark 10:35-52	Ps. 49:1-9
9-Mar	Num. 6:22-7:47	Mark 11	Ps. 49:10-20
10-Mar	Num. 7:48-8:4	Mark 12:1-27	Ps. 50:1-15
11-Mar	Num. 8:5-9:23	Mark 12:28-44	Ps. 50:16-23
12-Mar	Num. 10-11	Mark 13:1-8	Ps. 51:1-9
13-Mar	Num. 12-13	Mark 13:9-37	Ps. 51:10-19
14-Mar	Num. 14	Mark 14:1-31	Ps. 52
15-Mar	Num. 15	Mark 14:32-72	Ps. 53
16-Mar	Num. 16	Mark 15:1-32	Ps. 54
17-Mar	Num. 17-18	Mark 15:33-47	Ps. 55
18-Mar	Num. 19-20	Mark 16	Ps. 56:1-7
19-Mar	Num. 21:1-22:20	Luke 1:1-25	Ps. 56:8-13
20-Mar	Num. 22:21-23:30	Luke 1:26-56	Ps. 57
21-Mar	Num. 24-25	Luke 1:57-2:20	Ps. 58
22-Mar	Num. 26:1-27:11	Luke 2:21-38	Ps. 59:1-8

23-Mar	Num. 27:12-29:11	Luke 2:39-52	Ps. 59:9-17
24-Mar	Num. 29:12-30:16	Luke 3	Ps. 60:1-5
25-Mar	Num. 31	Luke 4	Ps. 60:6-12
26-Mar	Num. 32-33	Luke 5:1-16	Ps. 61
27-Mar	Num. 34-36	Luke 5:17-32	Ps. 62:1-6
28-Mar	Deut. 1:1-2:25	Luke 5:33-6:11	Ps. 62:7-12
29-Mar	Deut. 2:26-4:14	Luke 6:12-35	Ps. 63:1-5
30-Mar	Deut. 4:15-5:22	Luke 6:36-49	Ps. 63:6-11
31-Mar	Deut. 5:23-7:26	Luke 7:1-17	Ps. 64:1-5
1-Apr	Deut. 8-9	Luke 7:18-35	Ps. 64:6-10
2-Apr	Deut. 10-11	Luke 7:36-8:3	Ps. 65:1-8
3-Apr	Deut. 12-13	Luke 8:4-21	Ps. 65:9-13
4-Apr	Deut. 14:1-16:8	Luke 8:22-39	Ps. 66:1-7
5-Apr	Deut. 16:9-18:22	Luke 8:40-56	Ps. 66:8-15
6-Apr	Deut. 19:1-21:9	Luke 9:1-22	Ps. 66:16-20
7-Apr	Deut. 21:10-23:8	Luke 9:23-42	Ps. 67
8-Apr	Deut. 23:9-25:19	Luke 9:43-62	Ps. 68:1-6
9-Apr	Deut. 26:1-28:14	Luke 10:1-20	Ps. 68:7-14
10-Apr	Deut. 28:15-68	Luke 10:21-37	Ps. 68:15-19
11-Apr	Deut. 29-30	Luke 10:38-11:23	Ps. 68:20-27
12-Apr	Deut. 31:1-32:22	Luke 11:24-36	Ps. 68:28-35
13-Apr	Deut. 32:23-33:29	Luke 11:37-54	Ps. 69:1-9
14-Apr	Deut. 34-Josh. 2	Luke 12:1-15	Ps. 69:10-17
15-Apr	Josh. 3:1-5:12	Luke 12:16-40	Ps. 69:18-28
16-Apr	Josh. 5:13-7:26	Luke 12:41-48	Ps. 69:29-36
17-Apr	Josh. 8-9	Luke 12:49-59	Ps. 70
18-Apr	Josh. 10:1-11:15	Luke 13:1-21	Ps. 71:1-6
19-Apr	Josh. 11:16-13:33	Luke 13:22-35	Ps. 71:7-16
20-Apr	Josh. 14-16	Luke 14:1-15	Ps. 71:17-21
21-Apr	Josh. 17:1-19:16	Luke 14:16-35	Ps. 71:22-24
22-Apr	Josh. 19:17-21:42	Luke 15:1-10	Ps. 72:1-11
23-Apr	Josh. 21:43-22:34	Luke 15:11-32	Ps. 72:12-20
24-Apr	Josh. 23-24	Luke 16:1-18	Ps. 73:1-9
25-Apr	Judg. 1-2	Luke 16:19-17:10	Ps. 73:10-20
26-Apr	Judg. 3-4	Luke 17:11-37	Ps. 73:21-28
27-Apr	Judg. 5:1-6:24	Luke 18:1-17	Ps. 74:1-3
28-Apr	Judg. 6:25-7:25	Luke 18:18-43	Ps. 74:4-11
29-Apr	Judg. 8:1-9:23	Luke 19:1-28	Ps. 74:12-17
30-Apr	Judg. 9:24-10:18	Luke 19:29-48	Ps. 74:18-23
1-May	Judg. 11:1-12:7	Luke 20:1-26	Ps. 75:1-7
2-May	Judg. 12:8-14:20	Luke 20:27-47	Ps. 75:8-10

3-May	Judg. 15-16	Luke 21:1-19	Ps. 76:1-7
4-May	Judg. 17-18	Luke 21:20-22:6	Ps. 76:8-12
5-May	Judg. 19:1-20:23	Luke 22:7-30	Ps. 77:1-11
6-May	Judg. 20:24-21:25	Luke 22:31-54	Ps. 77:12-20
7-May	Ruth 1-2	Luke 22:55-23:25	Ps. 78:1-4
8-May	Ruth 3-4	Luke 23:26-24:12	Ps. 78:5-8
9-May	1 Sam. 1:1-2:21	Luke 24:13-53	Ps. 78:9-16
10-May	1 Sam. 2:22-4:22	John 1:1-28	Ps. 78:17-24
11-May	1 Sam. 5-7	John 1:29-51	Ps. 78:25-33
12-May	1 Sam. 8:1-9:26	John 2	Ps. 78:34-41
13-May	1 Sam. 9:27-11:15	John 3:1-22	Ps. 78:42-55
14-May	1 Sam. 12-13	John 3:23-4:10	Ps. 78:56-66
15-May	1 Sam. 14	John 4:11-38	Ps. 78:67-72
16-May	1 Sam. 15-16	John 4:39-54	Ps. 79:1-7
17-May	1 Sam. 17	John 5:1-24	Ps. 79:8-13
18-May	1 Sam. 18-19	John 5:25-47	Ps. 80:1-7
19-May	1 Sam. 20-21	John 6:1-21	Ps. 80:8-19
20-May	1 Sam. 22-23	John 6:22-42	Ps. 81:1-10
21-May	1 Sam. 24:1-25:31	John 6:43-71	Ps. 81:11-16
22-May	1 Sam. 25:32-27:12	John 7:1-24	Ps. 82
23-May	1 Sam. 28-29	John 7:25-8:11	Ps. 83
24-May	1 Sam. 30-31	John 8:12-47	Ps. 84:1-4
25-May	2 Sam. 1-2	John 8:48-9:12	Ps. 84:5-12
26-May	2 Sam. 3-4	John 9:13-34	Ps. 85:1-7
27-May	2 Sam. 5:1-7:17	John 9:35-10:10	Ps. 85:8-13
28-May	2 Sam. 7:18-10:19	John 10:11-30	Ps. 86:1-10
29-May	2 Sam. 11:1-12:25	John 10:31-11:16	Ps. 86:11-17
30-May	2 Sam. 12:26-13:39	John 11:17-54	Ps. 87
31-May	2 Sam. 14:1-15:12	John 11:55-12:19	Ps. 88:1-9
1-Jun	2 Sam. 15:13-16:23	John 12:20-43	Ps. 88:10-18
2-Jun	2 Sam. 17:1-18:18	John 12:44-13:20	Ps. 89:1-6
3-Jun	2 Sam. 18:19-19:39	John 13:21-38	Ps. 89:7-13
4-Jun	2 Sam. 19:40-21:22	John 14:1-17	Ps. 89:14-18
5-Jun	2 Sam. 22:1-23:7	John 14:18-15:27	Ps. 89:19-29
6-Jun	2 Sam. 23:8-24:25	John 16:1-22	Ps. 89:30-37
7-Jun	1 Kings 1	John 16:23-17:5	Ps. 89:38-52
8-Jun	1 Kings 2	John 17:6-26	Ps. 90:1-12
9-Jun	1 Kings 3-4	John 18:1-27	Ps. 90:13-17
10-Jun	1 Kings 5-6	John 18:28-19:5	Ps. 91:1-10
11-Jun	1 Kings 7	John 19:6-25a	Ps. 91:11-16
12-Jun	1 Kings 8:1-53	John 19:25b-42	Ps. 92:1-9

13-Jun	1 Kings 8:54-10:13	John 20:1-18	Ps. 92:10-15
14-Jun	1 Kings 10:14-11:43	John 20:19-31	Ps. 93
15-Jun	1 Kings 12:1-13:10	John 21	Ps. 94:1-11
16-Jun	1 Kings 13:11-14:31	Acts 1:1-11	Ps. 94:12-23
17-Jun	1 Kings 15:1-16:20	Acts 1:12-26	Ps. 95
18-Jun	1 Kings 16:21-18:19	Acts 2:1-21	Ps. 96:1-8
19-Jun	1 Kings 18:20-19:21	Acts2:22-41	Ps. 96:9-13
20-Jun	1 Kings 20	Acts 2:42-3:26	Ps. 97:1-6
21-Jun	1 Kings 21:1-22:28	Acts 4:1-22	Ps. 97:7-12
22-Jun	1 Kings 22:29- 2 Kings 1:18	Acts 4:23-5:11	Ps. 98
23-Jun	2 Kings 2-3	Acts 5:12-28	Ps. 99
24-Jun	2 Kings 4	Acts 5:29-6:15	Ps. 100
25-Jun	2 Kings 5:1-6:23	Acts 7:1-16	Ps. 101
26-Jun	2 Kings 6:24-8:15	Acts 7:17-36	Ps. 102:1-7
27-Jun	2 Kings 8:16-9:37	Acts 7:37-53	Ps. 102:8-17
28-Jun	2 Kings 10-11	Acts 7:54-8:8	Ps. 102:18-28
29-Jun	2 Kings 12-13	Acts 8:9-40	Ps. 103:1-9
30-Jun	2 Kings 14-15	Acts 9:1-16	Ps. 103:10-14
1-Jul	2 Kings 16-17	Acts 9:17-31	Ps. 103:15-22
2-Jul	2 Kings 18:1-19:7	Acts 9:32-10:16	Ps. 104:1-9
3-Jul	2 Kings 19:8-20:21	Acts 10:17-33	Ps. 104:10-23
4-Jul	2 Kings 21:1-22:20	Acts 10:34-11:18	Ps. 104: 24-30
5-Jul	2 Kings 23	Acts 11:19-12:17	Ps. 104:31-35
6-Jul	2 Kings 24-25	Acts 12:18-13:13	Ps. 105:1-7
7-Jul	1 Chron. 1-2	Acts 13:14-43	Ps. 105:8-15
8-Jul	1 Chron. 3:1-5:10	Acts 13:44-14:10	Ps. 105:16-28
9-Jul	1 Chron. 5:11-6:81	Acts 14:11-28	Ps. 105:29-36
10-Jul	1 Chron. 7:1-9:9	Acts 15:1-18	Ps. 105:37-45
11-Jul	1 Chron. 9:10-11:9	Acts 15:19-41	Ps. 106:1-12
12-Jul	1 Chron. 11:10-12:40	Acts 16:1-15	Ps. 106:13-27
13-Jul	1 Chron. 13-15	Acts 16:16-40	Ps. 106:28-33
14-Jul	1 Chron. 16-17	Acts 17:1-14	Ps. 106:34-43
15-Jul	1 Chron. 18-20	Acts 17:15-34	Ps. 106:44-48
16-Jul	1 Chron. 21-22	Acts 18:1-23	Ps. 107:1-9
17-Jul	1 Chron. 23-25	Acts 18:24-19:10	Ps. 107:10-16
18-Jul	1 Chron. 26-27	Acts 19:11-22	Ps. 107:17-32
19-Jul	1 Chron. 28-29	Acts 19:23-41	Ps. 107:33-38
20-Jul	2 Chron. 1-3	Acts 20:1-16	Ps. 107:39-43
21-Jul	2 Chron. 4:1-6:11	Acts 20:17-38	Ps. 108
22-Jul	2 Chron. 6:12-7:10	Acts 21:1-14	Ps. 109:1-20

23-Jul	2 Chron. 7:11-9:28	Acts 21:15-32	Ps. 109:21-31
24-Jul	2 Chron. 9:29-12:16	Acts 21:33-22:16	Ps. 110:1-3
25-Jul	2 Chron. 13-15	Acts 22:17-23:11	Ps. 110:4-7
26-Jul	2 Chron. 16-17	Acts 23:12-24:21	Ps. 111
27-Jul	2 Chron. 18-19	Acts 24:22-25:12	Ps. 112
28-Jul	2 Chron. 20-21	Acts 25:13-27	Ps. 113
29-Jul	2 Chron. 22-23	Acts 26	Ps. 114
30-Jul	2 Chron. 24:1-25:16	Acts 27:1-20	Ps. 115:1-10
31-Jul	2 Chron. 25:17-27:9	Acts 27:21-28:6	Ps. 115:11-18
1-Aug	2 Chron. 28:1-29:19	Acts 28:7-31	Ps. 116:1-5
2-Aug	2 Chron. 29:20-30:27	Rom. 1:1-17	Ps. 116:6-19
3-Aug	2 Chron. 31-32	Rom. 1:18-32	Ps. 117
4-Aug	2 Chron. 33:1-34:7	Rom. 2	Ps. 118:1-18
5-Aug	2 Chron. 34:8-35:19	Rom. 3:1-26	Ps. 118:19-23
6-Aug	2 Chron. 35:20-36:23	Rom. 3:27-4:25	Ps. 118:24-29
7-Aug	Ezra 1-3	Rom. 5	Ps. 119:1-8
8-Aug	Ezra 4-5	Rom. 6:1-7:6	Ps. 119:9-16
9-Aug	Ezra 6:1-7:26	Rom. 7:7-25	Ps. 119:17-32
10-Aug	Ezra 7:27-9:4	Rom. 8:1-27	Ps. 119:33-40
11-Aug	Ezra 9:5-10:44	Rom. 8:28-39	Ps. 119:41-64
12-Aug	Neh. 1:1-3:16	Rom. 9:1-18	Ps. 119:65-72
13-Aug	Neh. 3:17-5:13	Rom. 9:19-33	Ps. 119:73-80
14-Aug	Neh. 5:14-7:73	Rom. 10:1-13	Ps. 119:81-88
15-Aug	Neh. 8:1-9:5	Rom. 10:14-11:24	Ps. 119:89-104
16-Aug	Neh. 9:6-10:27	Rom. 11:25-12:8	Ps. 119:105-120
17-Aug	Neh. 10:28-12:26	Rom. 12:9-13:7	Ps. 119:121-128
18-Aug	Neh. 12:27-13:31	Rom. 13:8-14:12	Ps. 119:129-136
19-Aug	Esther 1:1-2:18	Rom. 14:13-15:13	Ps. 119:137-152
20-Aug	Esther 2:19-5:14	Rom. 15:14-21	Ps. 119:153-168
21-Aug	Esther. 6-8	Rom. 15:22-33	Ps. 119:169-176
22-Aug	Esther 9-10	Rom. 16	Ps. 120-122
23-Aug	Job 1-3	1 Cor. 1:1-25	Ps. 123
24-Aug	Job 4-6	1 Cor. 1:26-2:16	Ps. 124-125
25-Aug	Job 7-9	1 Cor. 3	Ps. 126-127
26-Aug	Job 10-13	1 Cor. 4:1-13	Ps. 128-129
27-Aug	Job 14-16	1 Cor. 4:14-5:13	Ps. 130
28-Aug	Job 17-20	1 Cor. 6	Ps. 131
29-Aug	Job 21-23	1 Cor. 7:1-16	Ps. 132
30-Aug	Job 24-27	1 Cor. 7:17-40	Ps. 133-134
31-Aug	Job 28-30	1 Cor. 8	Ps. 135
1-Sep	Job 31-33	1 Cor. 9:1-18	Ps. 136:1-9

2-Sep	Job 34-36	1 Cor. 9:19-10:13	Ps. 136:10-26
3-Sep	Job 37-39	1 Cor. 10:14-11:1	Ps. 137
4-Sep	Job 40-42	1 Cor. 11:2-34	Ps. 138
5-Sep	Eccles. 1:1-3:15	1 Cor. 12:1-26	Ps. 139:1-6
6-Sep	Eccles. 3:16-6:12	1 Cor. 12:27-13:13	Ps. 139:7-18
7-Sep	Eccles. 7:1-9:12	1 Cor. 14:1-22	Ps. 139:19-24
8-Sep	Eccles. 9:13-12:14	1 Cor. 14:23-15:11	Ps. 140:1-8
9-Sep	SS 1-4	1 Cor. 15:12-34	Ps. 140:9-13
10-Sep	SS 5-8	1 Cor. 15:35-58	Ps. 141
11-Sep	Isa. 1-2	1 Cor. 16	Ps. 142
12-Sep	Isa. 3-5	2 Cor. 1:1-11	Ps. 143:1-6
13-Sep	Isa. 6-8	2 Cor. 1:12-2:4	Ps. 143:7-12
14-Sep	Isa. 9-10	2 Cor. 2:5-17	Ps. 144
15-Sep	Isa. 11-13	2 Cor. 3	Ps. 145
16-Sep	Isa. 14-16	2 Cor. 4	Ps. 146
17-Sep	Isa. 17-19	2 Cor. 5	Ps. 147:1-11
18-Sep	Isa. 20-23	2 Cor. 6	Ps. 147:12-20
19-Sep	Isa. 24:1-26:19	2 Cor. 7	Ps. 148
20-Sep	Isa. 26:20-28:29	2 Cor. 8	Ps. 149-150
21-Sep	Isa. 29-30	2 Cor. 9	Prov. 1:1-9
22-Sep	Isa. 31-33	2 Cor. 10	Prov. 1:10-22
23-Sep	Isa. 34-36	2 Cor. 11	Prov. 1:23-26
24-Sep	Isa. 37-38	2 Cor. 12:1-10	Prov. 1:27-33
25-Sep	Isa. 39-40	2 Cor. 12:11-13:14	Prov. 2:1-15
26-Sep	Isa. 41-42	Gal. 1	Prov. 2:16-22
27-Sep	Isa. 43:1-44:20	Gal. 2	Prov. 3:1-12
28-Sep	Isa. 44:21-46:13	Gal. 3:1-18	Prov. 3:13-26
29-Sep	Isa. 47:1-49:13	Gal 3:19-29	Prov. 3:27-35
30-Sep	Isa. 49:14-51:23	Gal 4:1-11	Prov. 4:1-19
1-Oct	Isa. 52-54	Gal. 4:12-31	Prov. 4:20-27
2-Oct	Isa. 55-57	Gal. 5	Prov. 5:1-14
3-Oct	Isa. 58-59	Gal. 6	Prov. 5:15-23
4-Oct	Isa. 60-62	Eph. 1	Prov. 6:1-5
5-Oct	Isa. 63:1-65:16	Eph. 2	Prov. 6:6-19
6-Oct	Isa. 65:17-66:24	Eph. 3:1-4:16	Prov. 6:20-26
7-Oct	Jer. 1-2	Eph. 4:17-32	Prov. 6:27-35
8-Oct	Jer. 3:1-4:22	Eph. 5	Prov. 7:1-5
9-Oct	Jer. 4:23-5:31	Eph. 6	Prov. 7:6-27
10-Oct	Jer. 6:1-7:26	Phil. 1:1-26	Prov. 8:1-11
11-Oct	Jer. 7:26-9:16	Phil. 1:27-2:18	Prov. 8:12-21
12-Oct	Jer. 9:17-11:17	Phil 2:19-30	Prov. 8:22-36

13-Oct	Jer. 11:18-13:27	Phil. 3	Prov. 9:1-6
14-Oct	Jer. 14-15	Phil. 4	Prov. 9:7-18
15-Oct	Jer. 16-17	Col. 1:1-23	Prov. 10:1-5
16-Oct	Jer. 18:1-20:6	Col. 1:24-2:15	Prov. 10:6-14
17-Oct	Jer. 20:7-22:19	Col. 2:16-3:4	Prov. 10:15-26
18-Oct	Jer. 22:20-23:40	Col. 3:5-4:1	Prov. 10:27-32
19-Oct	Jer. 24-25	Col. 4:2-18	Prov. 11:1-11
20-Oct	Jer. 26-27	1 Thes. 1:1-2:8	Prov. 11:12-21
21-Oct	Jer. 28-29	1 Thes. 2:9-3:13	Prov. 11:22-26
22-Oct	Jer. 30:1-31:22	1 Thes. 4:1-5:11	Prov. 11:27-31
23-Oct	Jer. 31:23-32:35	1 Thes. 5:12-28	Prov. 12:1-14
24-Oct	Jer. 32:36-34:7	2 Thes. 1-2	Prov. 12:15-20
25-Oct	Jer. 34:8-36:10	2 Thes. 3	Prov. 12:21-28
26-Oct	Jer. 36:11-38:13	1 Tim. 1:1-17	Prov. 13:1-4
27-Oct	Jer. 38:14-40:6	1 Tim. 1:18-3:13	Prov. 13:5-13
28-Oct	Jer. 40:7-42:22	1 Tim. 3:14-4:10	Prov. 13:14-21
29-Oct	Jer. 43-44	1 Tim. 4:11-5:16	Prov. 13:22-25
30-Oct	Jer. 45-47	1 Tim. 5:17-6:21	Prov. 14:1-6
31-Oct	Jer. 48:1-49:6	2 Tim. 1	Prov. 14:7-22
1-Nov	Jer. 49:7-50:16	2 Tim. 2	Prov. 14:23-27
2-Nov	Jer. 50:17-51:14	2 Tim. 3	Prov. 14:28-35
3-Nov	Jer. 51:15-64	2 Tim. 4	Prov. 15:1-9
4-Nov	Jer. 52-Lam. 1	Ti. 1:1-9	Prov. 15:10-17
5-Nov	Lam. 2:1-3:38	Ti. 1:10-2:15	Prov. 15:18-26
6-Nov	Lam. 3:39-5:22	Ti. 3	Prov. 15:27-33
7-Nov	Ezek. 1:1-3:21	Philemon 1	Prov. 16:1-9
8-Nov	Ezek. 3:22-5:17	Heb. 1:1-2:4	Prov. 16:10-21
9-Nov	Ezek. 6-7	Heb. 2:5-18	Prov. 16:22-33
10-Nov	Ezek. 8-10	Heb. 3:1-4:3	Prov. 17:1-5
11-Nov	Ezek. 11-12	Heb. 4:4-5:10	Prov. 17:6-12
12-Nov	Ezek. 13-14	Heb. 5:11-6:20	Prov. 17:13-22
13-Nov	Ezek. 15:1-16:43	Heb. 7:1-28	Prov. 17:23-28
14-Nov	Ezek. 16:44-17:24	Heb. 8:1-9:10	Prov. 18:1-7
15-Nov	Ezek. 18-19	Heb. 9:11-28	Prov. 18:8-17
16-Nov	Ezek. 20	Heb. 10:1-25	Prov. 18:18-24
17-Nov	Ezek. 21-22	Heb. 10:26-39	Prov. 19:1-8
18-Nov	Ezek. 23	Heb. 11:1-31	Prov. 19:9-14
19-Nov	Ezek. 24-26	Heb. 11:32-40	Prov. 19:15-21
20-Nov	Ezek. 27-28	Heb. 12:1-13	Prov. 19:22-29
21-Nov	Ezek. 29-30	Heb. 12:14-29	Prov. 20:1-18
22-Nov	Ezek. 31-32	Heb. 13	Prov. 20:19-24

23-Nov	Ezek. 33:1-34:10	Jas. 1	Prov. 20:25-30
24-Nov	Ezek. 34:11-36:15	Jas. 2	Prov. 21:1-8
25-Nov	Ezek. 36:16-37:28	Jas. 3	Prov. 21:9-18
26-Nov	Ezek. 38-39	Jas. 4:1-5:6	Prov. 21:19-24
27-Nov	Ezek. 40	Jas. 5:7-20	Prov. 21:25-31
28-Nov	Ezek. 41:1-43:12	1 Pet. 1:1-12	Prov. 22:1-9
29-Nov	Ezek. 43:13-44:31	1 Pet. 1:13-2:3	Prov. 22:10-23
30-Nov	Ezek. 45-46	1 Pet. 2:4-17	Prov. 22:24-29
1-Dec	Ezek. 47-48	1 Pet. 2:18-3:7	Prov. 23:1-9
2-Dec	Dan. 1:1-2:23	1 Pet. 3:8-4:19	Prov. 23:10-16
3-Dec	Dan. 2:24-3:30	1 Pet. 5	Prov. 23:17-25
4-Dec	Dan. 4	2 Pet. 1	Prov. 23:26-35
5-Dec	Dan. 5	2 Pet. 2	Prov. 24:1-18
6-Dec	Dan. 6:1-7:14	2 Pet. 3	Prov. 24:19-27
7-Dec	Dan. 7:15-8:27	1 John 1:1-2:17	Prov. 24:28-34
8-Dec	Dan. 9-10	1 John 2:18-29	Prov. 25:1-12
9-Dec	Dan. 11-12	1 John 3:1-12	Prov. 25:13-17
10-Dec	Hos. 1-3	1 John 3:13-4:16	Prov. 25:18-28
11-Dec	Hos. 4-6	1 John 4:17-5:21	Prov. 26:1-16
12-Dec	Hos. 7-10	2 John	Prov. 26:17-21
13-Dec	Hos. 11-14	3 John	Prov. 26:22-27:9
14-Dec	Joel 1:1-2:17	Jude	Prov. 27:10-17
15-Dec	Joel 2:18-3:21	Rev. 1:1-2:11	Prov. 27:18-27
16-Dec	Amos 1:1-4:5	Rev. 2:12-29	Prov. 28:1-8
17-Dec	Amos 4:6-6:14	Rev. 3	Prov. 28:9-16
18-Dec	Amos 7-9	Rev. 4:1-5:5	Prov. 28:17-24
19-Dec	Obad-Jonah	Rev. 5:6-14	Prov. 28:25-28
20-Dec	Mic. 1:1-4:5	Rev. 6:1-7:8	Prov. 29:1-8
21-Dec	Mic. 4:6-7:20	Rev. 7:9-8:13	Prov. 29:9-14
22-Dec	Nah. 1-3	Rev. 9-10	Prov. 29:15-23
23-Dec	Hab. 1-3	Rev. 11	Prov. 29:24-27
24-Dec	Zeph. 1-3	Rev. 12	Prov. 30:1-6
25-Dec	Hag. 1-2	Rev. 13:1-14:13	Prov. 30:7-16
26-Dec	Zech. 1-4	Rev. 14:14-16:3	Prov. 30:17-20
27-Dec	Zech. 5-8	Rev. 16:4-21	Prov. 30:21-28
28-Dec	Zech. 9-11	Rev. 17:1-18:8	Prov. 30:29-33
29-Dec	Zech. 12-14	Rev. 18:9-24	Prov. 31:1-9
30-Dec	Mal. 1-2	Rev. 19-20	Prov. 31:10-17
31-Dec	Mal. 3-4	Rev. 21-22	Prov. 31:18-31

Also from Barbour Publishing. . .

On My Way Home

Limitless Grace

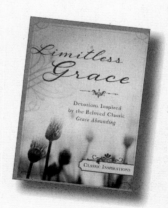